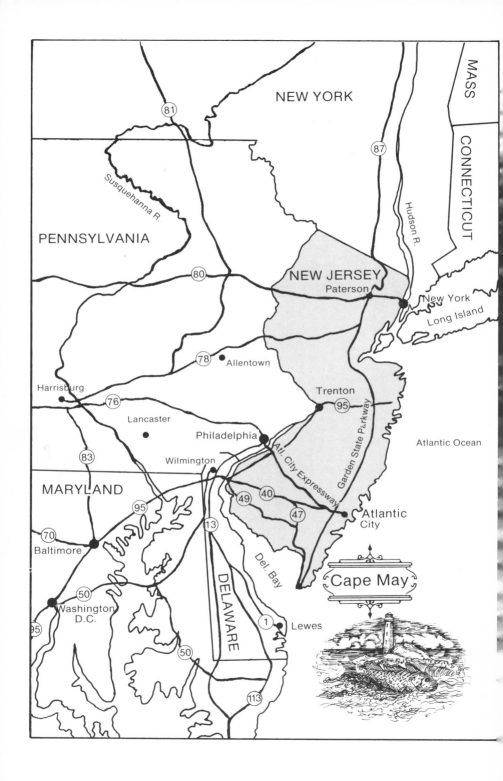

NEW YORK

MASS

CONNECTICUT

Susquehanna R.

PENNSYLVANIA

81

80

NEW JERSEY

Paterson

Hudson R.

87

New York

Long Island

78

Allentown

Harrisburg

76

Trenton

95

Garden State Parkway

Lancaster

Philadelphia

Atl. City Expressway

Atlantic Ocean

83

Wilmington

MARYLAND

95

49 40

47

Atlantic
City

13

70

Baltimore

Del. Bay

DELAWARE

Cape May

50

Washington
D.C.

95

50

1

Lewes

113

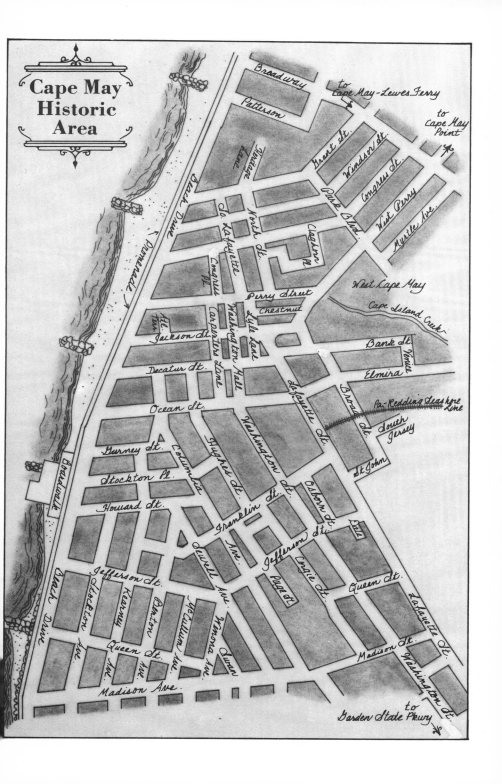

Cape May
Historic
Area

VICTORIAN HOLIDAYS

An Illustrated Guide to Favorite

GUEST HOUSES
BED & BREAKFAST INNS
and
RESTAURANTS
of
CAPE MAY, NEW JERSEY
America's Oldest Seashore Resort

by
Marsha Cudworth
&
Howard Michaels

Drawings by Marsha Cudworth
Photographs by Howard Michaels

New York, New York
1984

This book is dedicated to
Robert and Fran Malina,
whose encouragement and generosity
has made this publication possible.

CONTENTS

COTTAGES ON COLUMBIA AVENUE.

Preface

Cape May . . . "The playground for Presidents; a gingerbread spa-by-the sea; an entire city designated a National Historic Landmark; the nation's oldest seaside resort . . ."

The 20th century visitor, familiar with these quotes, comes to Cape May with a particular sense of anticipation and historical curiosity. Using many of the same routes traveled by the earliest visitors, today's tourist comes from the north, west and south— through the virtually unchanged Pine Barrens of New Jersey, past century-old vegetable and dairy farms and down main streets of little known towns.

The over-land route finally ends as the highway reaches up and dips down over the bridge leading into Cape May. Tiny wooden structures and old fishing piers line the creek. There is now sky and water all around, and it is easy to imagine the days when Cape May was known as Cape Island.

A strange transformation takes place as one enters a town that might have been brushed in by a 19th century artist—the car becomes a hindrance—a trapping of the 20th century that somehow feels out of place. *This is a town to get close to* and the best way to absorb its presence is to walk.

Slow down and savor the unique scene while traveling under a canopy of 100 year old trees; past picket fences, lacy shuttered windows and wide wrap-around verandas, filled with rocking chairs and ocean breezes. Gaze upward at graceful turrets and cupolas, topping wooden clapboard homes. Whimsical gazebos and lovely gardens bursting with yellow tiger-lilies and blue-violet hydrangea abound.

Discover the gentler pace of a proud, historic town whose graceful styles of yesteryear are alive at every turn of the corner.

Cape Island
∽
The Cape May of Yesteryear

There are many seaside resort towns in the United States today, but few can compare with the rich, historical background of Cape May, New Jersey. An understanding of its phenomenal rediscovery must begin with an appreciation of its past.

Early records indicate that a band of peace loving Lenni-Lenape Indians sought relief from the summer heat on Cape Island's shores, and were there when the first white men sailed their ships along the coast and into the bay.

In 1620, the same year the Pilgrims landed on Plymouth Rock, Captain Cornelius Jacobsen Mey explored New Jersey and the Delaware Bay area. He declared the climate of these fruitful lands as good as his homeland of Holland and named Cape May for himself.

Many of the first settlers were whalers from New England and it has been reputed that more descendents of the Mayflower Pilgrims lived in Cape May than anywhere else!

Its ensuing popularity as a resort may have begun as early as 1766 when Robert Parsons placed an advertisement in the Pennsylvania Gazette, offering for sale his 254 acre plantation situated one mile from the resort of Cape May, "which would be very convenient for taking in such people (tourists)". However, it was not until the early 1800's that visitors would be drawn in great numbers from

Philadelphia, as well as from other cities in Pennsylvania, Delaware and Maryland. Cape May was also a great attraction for rich plantation owners and other members of "Southern Society". Interestingly, the Cape was considered to be part of the *South* and actually fell below a projected Mason-Dixon line.

The earliest travelers from Philadelphia came by stagecoach and took as long as two days to traverse the sandy roads of South Jersey. Others came by sailing sloops, steamboats and packet boats. By the mid-1800's, steamboat lines offered a daily run from Philadelphia to Cape May for $6 round trip, including meals. Steamtrains soon took care of the overland journey and carried passengers from Philadelphia and points further south by way of Baltimore.

Right from the start, there seemed to be an abundance of visitors and a shortage of accommodations. Private boarding houses soon gave way to licensed "public houses" which were little more than barn-like dormitories, partitioned with curtains for sleeping: men on one side, women on the other.

The segregation of ladies and gents also extended to their swimming hours: a red flag signaled the men to the water; a white flag, the ladies. Bathers of this era wore an abundance of clothing into the ocean—tunics, pants, skirts, white collars and wristbands, stockings, bathing shoes and even straw hats! All this for "modesty's sake" and to avoid the sun. Tanned skin was an indication of the lower class who had to work outside during daytime hours.

During the midday heat, guests withdrew to the *public* rooms of their establishments—to the dining areas, game rooms, the card room, the writing room, the lobby, and to the most favorite spot of all—the veranda, where society could see and be seen. Clothes were of the utmost importance and were changed several times a day. Men wore three piece suits, top hats and carried canes. The women dressed in voluminous skirts (with waist-clinching corsets underneath) and carried parasols to protect their alabaster complexions.

Members of this fashionable elite strolled along the avenues or went for carriage rides on the hard packed sand. While ladies played ten-pin or cooled themselves on the open verandas, the men gambled in clubs, sharpened their skills in shooting galleries, or bet on horse races on the beach.

Cape May of the mid-nineteenth century saw a procession of presidents and statesmen visiting the resort—Franklin Pierce being the first president, followed by Chester A. Arthur and Ulysses S. Grant. Senator Henry Clay came in 1847 seeking solace following the death of his son. Twelve years before he was to become president, Congressman Abraham Lincoln, on a Whig campaign tour, checked into The Mansion House with his wife. Cape May also saw the likes of John Phillip Sousa, as he played a newly-composed march called "Congress Hall" on the lawn of that famous hotel which still stands today. The list of dignitaries grew with visits from Empress Carlotta, British actress Lily Langtry, writer Bret Harte and Clara Barton.

The golden age of grandeur reached ultimate heights with the heralded opening of The Mount Vernon, billed in The *Illustrated London News* on September 17, 1853 as a "palatial building far exceeding any hotel in England." When completed, it would accommodate 3,500 guests and hold place-settings for 2,500. The four story hotel had miles of balconies and verandas that wrapped around its exterior and was entirely lit by gas manufactured on its premises. On September 5, 1856, with only the final wing to be completed, the grand structure was found to be on fire. Within an hour and a half, it had burned to the ground.

Understandably, with prevailing high winds and little fire-fighting equipment on hand, blazes led to disastrous results, often destroying large sections of the town. The largest of these, in 1878, took with it the entire hotel district and substantially reduced the town's capacity to accommodate the vast number of visitors to Cape May. Although unfortunate, the fires provided fresh opportunities for new construction. During the 60's, 70's and 80's, hundreds of buildings were fabricated in every major architectural style of the Victorian era.

COLUMBIA AVENUE.   CAPE MAY, N. J.

OCEAN STREET.   CAPE MAY, N. J.

Contributing to this building boom were the wealthy Philadelphian "Main Liners", the owners of the excursion steamboats and railroads, rich merchants, bankers and the like, who were all displeased with overflowing hotels and crowds. They secured the best architects, builders and carpenters and commissioned them to create *private* summer residences—as large and as fashionable as money could buy! These new wooden structures exuberantly competed with each other for the most lavish ornamentation— latticework, scrolls and frets, brackets and bargeboards. Each architectural detail was painted a different color, to accentuate the skillful craftsmanship.

During the summers of 1890-91, President Benjamin Harrison and his wife spent much time in a private cottage at Cape May Point, owned by his Postmaster General, John Wanamaker (the Philadelphia department store magnate). Wanamaker was one of the founders of Cape May Point. The President set up his working

headquarters in Congress Hall (which was the resort's most famous hotel of that time), thus establishing the Summer White House concept.

At the turn of the century (1903), crowds of 20,000 waited all week to witness Henry Ford's beach skimmer compete with the world's top race car drivers in a week-long racing event.

Fires continued sporadically and the town still had no appreciable fire-fighting equipment. Tourists grew apprehensive as they were packed into overflowing wooden hotels. Soon, newly installed train lines and the advent of the automobile lured society to vacation at some of the more modern resorts, such as Atlantic City, further north. Cape May's golden age declined; with a brief revival during Prohibition with its bootlegging and rum-running. Following the roar of the 20's, the seaside town evolved into another sleepy South Jersey community with the yet-unrecognized distinction of having the greatest collection of late 19th century buildings in the United States today.

Cape May Today
∽
A Modern Renaissance

ow does an entire town get to be a National Historic Landmark? Through years of effort by people such as Caroline Pitts who, with a handful of concerned preservationists, fought off the "tear it down and put up a parking lot" philosophy of urban renewal. Her exhaustive fifteen year house-by-house research to catalog the town's vintage structures stirred local activists to organize an historical renewal conference, sponsored by the National Trust for Historic Preservation. Outspoken preservationists ran for official city positions on "historic value" issues and won.

Seven years of documentation by architects, students, historians and photographs from the University of Pennsylvania produced detailed drawings of historically significant houses, churches, cottages and hotels that are now deposited in the Library of Congress.

Residents began to realize the historic and esthetic worth of their Victorian properties and began to make repairs and impressive restorations of their own.

Townspeople supported a campaign to turn their run-down Washington Street business district into a Victorian pedestrian mall. Enlightened and enthused, culture buffs created the Mid-Atlantic Center for the Arts (MAC). Their first project was to secure a grant for the restoration of a deserted 1881 estate once owned by Dr. Emlen Physick. Under the leadership of Mayor Bruce Minnix, MAC raised enough money to match the grant and through the effort of many concerned citizens, the property has been refurbished and fully restored to its former splendour, housing a museum and cultural center. The success of the Physick Estate Restoration Project may have been the example which accelerated the Victorian Renaissance of Cape May.

TURN OF THE CENTURY—WASHINGTON STREET

oday, more and more vintage private residences are being bought up by a new, young breed of innkeepers and restaurant owners, who have chosen to settle in Cape May for a variety of reasons: a personal desire to own an old home and live in a small community; to get involved in major historical restoration and preservation and also to perform some kind of public service. They come from many different professional backgrounds, yet all seem to share a common bond—a genuine love for old things and an extreme sensitivity to preserve whatever is left of the past.

Presently, the fruits of this quiet boom are clearly evident in the restoration of buildings to be used as guesthouses and restaurants, as well as private residences. Most obvious are the freshly painted multi-colored exteriors, resurrecting the "true Victorian palette" and highlighting the exquisite architectural details which were hidden for years under layers of white paint.

Laborers with special skills are finding work. Carpenters trace and replace (or create anew) gingerbread bric-a-brac trim. Tin and slate roofers are repairing with renewed vigor. Fine furniture restorers remove layers of paint and varnish, making ready antique furnishings for new guesthouse rooms.

Owners of these historical buildings are deeply involved in full-scale restoration and maintenance. Problems ranging from bookkeeping to engineering have forced many into becoming the proverbial jack-of-all-trades. In almost all instances, the person who greets guests at the door, takes the luggage, cooks the breakfast and makes the beds, is the owner. Although immersed in this heavy schedule of greeting, cooking and cleaning, proprietors seem happy to take time to talk about the history of their house and the restorative work that was put into it.

Each inn and restaurant has its own personality and unique qualities. Some are devoted strictly to 19th century furnishings and maintaining a museum-like ambience, where genteel guests can eat and sleep Victorian. Others are more country-like, combining periods of the old and the new in a more casual atmosphere. All take pride in getting to know their guests and anticipating their needs.

Hopefully, this book will give the reader a clear picture of each guesthouse and restaurant, which were chosen for their intrinsic charm based on architectural style, history, furnishings, reputation of personal service and excellence in food preparation. Descriptive information contained herein has been gleaned from extensive interviews with innkeepers and restaurant owners, as well as overnight visits by the authors to each guesthouse and bed & breakfast inn. These visits took place during the extended season from April to November and included the enjoyable sampling of breakfasts, brunches, lunches and dinners at the restaurants and inns.

Most conveniently, Cape May is within a four hour drive from many of the East Coast's major cities—New York, Philadelphia, Washington, D.C., Baltimore and Wilmington. However, before embarking on a spur-of-the-moment vacation weekend, please note that *reservations are an absolute necessity*. Most inns have under ten rooms each and many have established clientele who have booked and paid for rooms in advance. We suggest that you inquire early in the spring (by phone or letter) about room availability for the inns that interest you. During the height of the summer season and on holiday weekends, most guesthouses require either a two or three day minimum stay, with a room deposit in advance. Families with young children are wise to inquire ahead of time to see if the establishment of their choice accommodates young children.

The increased popularity of bed and breakfast inns and guesthouses has substantially lengthened the season. Many inns stay open all year and provide charming fall and winter retreats with considerable ease in securing a room. Again, we suggest calling in advance; some may close during the slower months of January and February.

In this second edition, we have tried to indicate the most recent room rates, which have been quoted for double occupancy. Single guests may take advantage of special rates. Most inns offer discounts for extended and off-season stays. Although every effort has been made to represent each establishment as accurately as possible, we must remind readers that rates and schedules are subject to change.

Staying at one of Cape May's Victorian guesthouses or bed and breakfast inns is a refreshing change from today's fast-paced world. Be reminded that these inns are unlike today's motels. The absence of television, telephones and air conditioners in every room may be a welcome relief for some, but a requirement of others.

However, the recent popularity of this type of accommodation has shown that today's traveler is having a real romance with the past and clearly prefers to exchange a few modern conveniences for personal attention and care.

In an age where computerized and systemized accommodations and restaurants have reached new heights, we salute the integrity of those establishments included in this book who, in seeking to preserve the past, have created an environment of warm hospitality and real comfort for the traveler of today.

Guesthouses
and
Bed & Breakfast
Inns

 # The Dormer House International

 uiet streets surround the large corner on which the Dormer House International stands. Innkeepers Peg and Bill Madden have completely encircled their rambling house with beautiful living things—Japanese pine trees, climbing vines and flowering hedges. Colorful summer gardens, a spacious lawn, and urns of flowers line the front and side entrances. Birdbaths and feeders amidst all this natural beauty make a perfect haven for birds and butterflies.

Stepping onto the front porch, visitors are usually greeted by the Madden's friendly and protective dog, Pixie. A glimpse through the door reveals a lovely side porch enclosed in glass and filled from top to bottom with potted geraniums, ferns and summer wicker furniture. This very festive scene in shades of red, green and white invites one to come in and absorb the solarium atmosphere.

Once inside, Pixie becomes your friend and welcomes her new guests with a wag of the tail. Almost immediately the innkeepers appear, coming down from their second floor apartment to greet visitors. The Maddens bought their spacious twenty-one room house over three years ago and receive guests year 'round. Peg relates that the Jacoby family was the original owner at the turn of the century. Mr. Jacoby built it as a one-family summer home with servants' quarters in the rear. He had lots of children and grandchildren to accommodate, and his family filled up the three floors of rooms!

1

Today, the Dormer House is the Madden's private residence, with seven spacious guest apartment accommodations with full-size and studio kitchens. "Our regular guests are mostly families with children, and surprisingly, couples who enjoy spending time together doing some serious gourmet cooking!" exclaims Peg. Kitchens are equipped with all the basics for cooking and serving simple to fancy meals. Serious cooks might bring some table linens and favorite cooking accessories of their own.

The guest apartments located on all three floors of the large building are sparkling clean, and freshly painted. Rooms are furnished with nice combinations of old and new: nostalgic painted wooden chests and dressers, vanity tables with mirrors, lots of antique wicker and slipcovered armchairs and sofas.

Apartment No. 1 is graced with two elegant marble fireplaces and the bath in Apartment No. 2 has marble walls and floor. The original owner had a marble business in Philadelphia and spared no expense in using quantities of it in his home. Even out-of-doors, the front and side entrances are provided with heavy slabs of marble at curbside, which were probably used to mark the spot for dismounting from a horse!

In addition to the lovely solarium on the side of the Dormer House International, guests may use the house's "lobby" to meet and greet fellow guests. Noteworthy here is the exquisite stained glass panel tucked in a corner, and a massive fireplace and mantel hewn out of what looks to be a soft red sandstone. The sofa on the opposite wall is a perfect fireside spot to curl up with a good book.

Recently, the Maddens decided to officially add another word to the name of their guesthouse, changing it from the Dormer House to the Dormer House International. A starter collection of foreign flags from Ireland, Germany and Canada fly side by side from the front porch. (Bill is of Irish descent, Peg is German and they've hosted many Canadian visitors.) The Maddens relate that this is only the beginning—they hope to add more flags as time goes on. "We've changed our name because we love having foreign visitors and we do have lots of guests from various countries staying with us," stated Peg with a sincere smile.

Reflecting back several years, she adds, "Even though we've never formally operated a guesthouse until now, our house always seemed like one!" In explanation, the Maddens disclosed that they've raised five children who are now all on their own. Over the years, they have also opened their home to over thirty foster children; hosted three exchange students from Ethiopia; sponsored three young men from Vietnam after the war; and most recently, taken in three Cuban refugees.

Peg and Bill Madden are rare innkeepers whose lovely guest home reflects their own sense of inner peace. There is a real love of people here—young and old and in-between. Still smiling, Peg concludes, "Our message is that this is our home, not a motel . . . the atmosphere is peaceful . . . I love the flowers, a sense of order, a place that is quiet."

THE DORMER HOUSE INTERNATIONAL, 800 Columbia Avenue, Cape May, N.J. 08204 (609) 884-7446. Bill and Peg Madden, Innkeepers. A massive turn-of-the-century home with 7 guest apartments equipped with modern kitchen facilities. Open to guests year 'round. Individual apartments can accommodate up to 6 people. Apartment rentals do not include linens or maid service. Coin-operated laundry; cable TV hook-up (please bring your own TV set); bicycle rental available. Linens supplied by house for $6 per bed per visit. A detailed description of each apartment available by mail. Nice touches: Bowls and vases of fresh flowers are everywhere; garden views from windows of all exposures; hibachis and charcoal for picnics are provided.

The Windward House

he Windward House is a big old family seashore cottage sitting right in the heart of the historic district on busy Jackson Street. Built in the cedar shingle style of the 1890's, this dwelling has the amusing feature of 27 windows in various sizes and shapes on its exterior west wall! By mid-June, the green and white striped awnings roll down, the veranda is filled with wicker furniture and the tiny formal garden out front is blooming. Guests can just settle themselves down in one of those old-fashioned rockers—complete with a plumpy chintz pillow—and watch the comings and goings at the Mad Batter outdoor café across the street.

Stepping inside from that great people-watching porch, guests get a clue of what's in store within, as they pass through two massive solid-oak doors with circular and stained glass windows. The parlour is large and homey, filled with Victorian chaises, golden oak furniture, a cozy fireplace and lots of family momentos. Immediately, guests can feel that big, old, comfortable house atmosphere which owners Owen and Sandy Miller just love, and is why they recently decided to make this their permanent, year-round home.

(For years, the Millers operated the Windward House full-time only during the summer months and as a weekend retreat during the rest of the year.) Formerly residing the rest of the time in Bucks County, Pennsylvania, Owen worked as the Director of Training and Education for the Philadelphia National Bank, while Sandy alternated innkeeping duties with teaching elementary school.

The Millers purchased this home from Tom and Sue Carroll who ran it as the original Mainstay guesthouse back in the mid-70's. In May 1977, Sandy, Owen and son Owen Jr. moved in, changed the name to the Windward House (owing to their love of the sea and sailing), and began furnishing the rooms. Being a private residence, as well as a guesthouse, the Millers have made use of many family heirloom pieces which are spread throughout the inn.

Each of the seven guestrooms are color coordinated and each has a special theme reflected by distinct period furnishings. The Jenny Lind room, in shades of green, is filled with whimsical spool furniture. A most charming handmade quilt, appliqued with demure calico cats is tucked away, posing as an extra blanket on the top shelf of the closet. Corner windows provide two tiny glimpses of the ocean. The rosy Cottage Room features two double brass beds, a cottage bureau, curved windows and French doors which open to the second floor porch.

Guests staying in the Chippendale Room can enjoy a 1918 solid mahogany set of that style which Sandy's parents had made when they were first married. Through a little research, Sandy discovered that one of the strongest influences on Victorian furniture design was from the Chippendale era.

Additional guestrooms with names like the Renaissance Room, Wicker Room and Empire Room are all well-appointed and give hint to the furnishings within.

On the way down, guests can admire the grand staircase with its heart-shaped cutout designs or take the rear stairwell that leads to a small portrait gallery, which traces Owen and Sandy's history through some interesting family photographs.

The Windward House is also one of the few old homes to retain a number of stained and leaded glass windows, which were so popular at the turn of the century. Built in 1905, on the verge of the post-Victorian era, the house structurally contains many Victorian characteristics: the back stairwell leading from the original kitchen in the basement to the maid's quarters on the third floor; upper and lower porches; central hall concept; large windows and lots of oak throughout.

A unique feature of the Windward House is that it opens its doors to bicycle groups, a tradition started by Tom Carroll and carried on here during the off-season months. By putting cots in every room and allowing sleeping bags on the floor, the Millers can accommodate up to 35 guest bikers, and if necessary, make alternate arrangements for larger groups. The congenial nature of the Millers welcomes church groups, and with advance notice, does not discourage other traveling clubs to come by for a restful stay at the Windward.

THE WINDWARD HOUSE, 24 Jackson Street, Cape May, N.J. 08204, (609) 884-3368; Owen and Sandy Miller, Innkeepers. A turn-of-the-century seashore cottage with seven guestrooms and a two-bedroom English apartment with kitchen and private entrance. Will be open all year after July 3, 1983. Breakfast served except during July and August. Five guestrooms each have private baths and small refrigerators. Third floor bedrooms share a bath, a generous refrigerator and a rear sunporch. Well-behaved children permitted. Nice touches: Sun/shade porches at all three levels. Several bikes for free use; also available for guests' conveniences—clocks, clothes iron, games and a large collection of books of the Victorian period. Occasional visits by Sandy's 91-year old father, who shares some wonderful personal reminiscences.

 # Poor Richard's Inn

n 1882, George Hildreth built a private home next door to his Wyoming Hotel. One hundred years have gone by since then, but not much has changed on Jackson Street. The Wyoming Hotel is now known as the Carroll Villa and the Hildreth House still remains, lovingly restored and presently owned by Richard Samuelson and Harriett Sosson. Poor Richard's Inn, as it is now named, is a country Victorian guesthouse at its best; wonderfully eclectic with charming handmade touches everywhere.

Harriett has painstakingly covered most bedroom walls and some ceilings with flowery and calico printed wallpapers. Small wooden chests tucked in corners have been painted with scenes by Richard. The six guestrooms are furnished with a collection of personal styles; carved wooden headboards, country-painted furniture, patchwork quilts, caned rocking chairs and lots of plants. A shared bath on the second floor features a footed tub and creamy white porcelain pedestal sink. The third floor rooms all have dormer

windows and a rear sitting room features a small library and a refrigerator for guests.

Long hallways are hung with antique quilts and rooms are lined with original artwork, antique prints and photographs. Harriett has created a most amusing collection of collages featuring a juxta-position of famous characters, such as Mona Lisa, George Washington and the Statue of Liberty, among others. Richard's large abstracted landscape canvases add intrigue and a touch of 20th century to the old.

Architecturally, Poor Richard's Inn is a Victorian's dream. Listed on the National Register of Historic Places, the exterior of the house has been restored to its original beauty. The mansard roof has 1600 pieces of replaced slate; the terra-cotta color of the slate (which differed from the original) inspired Richard and Harriett to use a high contrast multi-colored paint scheme to accentuate each of the

architectural details. The effect is wonderfully reminiscent of San Francisco's "Painted Ladies."

Poor Richard's Inn is a guesthouse with rooms that range from singles to apartment suites that are bright and homey. As Richard puts it, "We don't pretend to offer a transcendental weekend into the past. Our beds are comfortable; we offer plenty of ice for socializing and enjoying the scene on busy Jackson Street." Despite the absence of a formal sitting room inside, the upper and lower porches, complete with rocking chairs, provide guests with a view of the ocean, and yes, even a tiny glimpse back into a time when the Seven Sister Cottages across the way were filled with vacationing Victorians.

POOR RICHARD'S INN, 17 Jackson Street, Cape May, N.J. 08204, (609) 884-3536. Listed on the National Register of Historic Places. Richard Samuelson and Harriett Sosson, Innkeepers. A country Victorian guesthouse with six rooms and two apartments. Open April 1 thru October. Guestrooms share bath. Well behaved children allowed; no pets. Nice touches: Lots of original artwork by the artists-in-residence; two thoroughly affectionate and charming pet cats to entertain guests.

The Holly House

ape May's former mayor Bruce Minnix, and his wife Corinne, were loyal guests of this Victorian guesthouse throughout the 50's. The Minnix's stayed here on their wedding trip and were drawn back each summer by the house's family atmosphere and its close proximity to the beach. When the owners decided to sell in 1962, Bruce and Corinne purchased the property, moved in and continued to accommodate guests of their own at a time when visitors to Cape May were seldom seen before July 4th or after Labor Day.

The Holly House is one in a row of Victorian cottages, affectionately named "The Seven Sisters", at the foot of Jackson Street. These identical houses were built in the Renaissance Revival style by the well-known 19th century architect, Stephen Decatur Button.

Well informed about the history of his property, Bruce relates that his home and its sisters were erected on what once was the general site of several ill-fated, but increasingly elaborate hotels, all named "The Atlantic". The Atlantic Hall (1800), the New Atlantic (1842) and the second New Atlantic (1869) all succumbed to fires. The Holly House and sisters were built here a bit later, circa 1891, during a high point of Cape May popularity. The Industrial Revolution sent thousands of well-to-do vacationers to southern New Jersey's "cool Cape May" and overflowing hotels led the rich to seek alternate accommodations. Thus, the era of the "summer cottage" was born.

Built as rental properties, the formal exteriors of the Seven Sisters were typical of a more urban design which was originally set in stone, but adapted to wood for their seaside setting.

A number of unique characteristics distinguish the cottages from their contemporaries in Cape May. Five of the seven structures turn their backs to busy Jackson Street and all share an interior courtyard facing the Atlantic Ocean. Seemingly identical, the Seven Sister Guesthouse, which is the closest to the ocean, was built to stand two and one-half feet smaller than the Holly House on the opposite end. The effect was to override the laws of diminishing perspective, so when viewed from the beach, all houses appear to be the same size! Another feature involves a story about a German carpenter who came to Cape May and built ten circular staircases in

one summer, then returned to Germany. It is believed that seven of these staircases are located in the Seven Sisters (the others are elsewhere in town). The three-story beauty at the Holly House is certainly an architectural and visual highpoint of its interior.

Guests entering from what seems to be the rear of the house, find themselves in a parlour-sitting room with a mix of contemporary and period pieces in a setting of off-white and warm earth colors. The focal point of the parlour is the original coal-grate fireplace. Comfortable sofas and armchairs all around provide guests with a perfect spot to settle down for a fireside chat and a sip of brandy, perhaps with a charming innkeeper and some of the other guests.

Five bright and airy guestrooms located on the second and third floors are filled with comfortable beds and functional pieces of restored furniture. Both Bruce and Corinne have collected many original prints and paintings and like to "redecorate" by changing the artwork on the walls. With a chuckle, Bruce relates, "We don't have any museum pieces here because basically I'm a klutz!" He adds that they've always objected to the house that looks like a magazine ad, and that he and Corinne do not operate on the plane of some of the more opulent Victorian guesthouses in the neighborhood. This attitude creates a very relaxing vacation for guests and allows for families with children over three years of age to enjoy one of Cape May's historical houses.

Operating their guesthouse since the early 60's, the Minnix's are

old hands at the trade. Bruce amusingly refers to themselves as the grandparents of the guesthouse renaissance in Cape May.

Concerned and involved with the many problems of historic preservation, Bruce ran for mayor in 1972 and won. During his term, he worked with many of the town's original preservationists who were concerned for Cape May's Victorian heritage. Their projects included securing a grant to turn the Physick Estate into a museum and cultural center; the revitalization of the Mid-Atlantic Center for the Arts (MAC) which began 3-day Victorian weekends; walking tours of the town and trolley car rides through the historic district. By the time Minnix's term ended, the entire city had been designated a National Historic Landmark by the Federal government.

Today, Bruce commutes to New York to his job as a television director for popular soap operas, but he still is involved with MAC and the continuing problems of historic preservation. Home on week-ends, he gives a delightful walking tour of the historic district; his narration filled with all the serious facts of Cape May's architectural gems sprinkled with amusing anecdotes of Victorian life.

Working on a small restoration project of their own, several years ago the Minnix's purchased the property adjoining the Seven Sisters' shared courtyard. A tiny group of structures was erected there and rented out to summer businesses to help pay off the mortgage. Bruce states, "In effect, when the property is paid off, the concession stands will "self-destruct" and back come the lawns and gardens!" Their plan is to recreate the Atlantic Terrace shared by the Seven Sister cottages in the late 1800's. A lovely and fitting proposal that will be worth waiting for!

———————————•◆•———————————

THE HOLLY HOUSE, 20 Jackson Street, Cape May, N.J. 08204; (609) 884-7365. Corinne and Bruce Minnix, Innkeepers. A Victorian cottage row house, one of the "Seven Sisters" individually listed on the National Register of Historic Places. Five guestrooms share two full baths with showers. Open all year. Children over 3 welcome, no pets. Nice touches: Ocean view front porch with swing and rockers; guesthouse specifically planned for informal comfort.

The Seventh Sister

 request for a room with a view would be easy to accommodate at this oceanside guesthouse; this inn has the advantageous position of being the "Sister" closest to the beach. Owners Joanne and Bob Myers operate their year 'round guesthouse-home as a means to live near the sea and to do restoration.

In contrast to the Victoriana and numerous antique-filled inns in Cape May, the Seventh Sister offers an absolutely unique atmosphere of simplicity, befitting its setting of sand, sea and sky.

Each room is individually designed around the original paintings of owner-operator Joanne Echevarria Myers, whose themes include immense lily-blooms and Victorian architectural details. There is much to admire here—live plants thrive on the incredible light and an extensive collection of seashells provide inspiration for the delicate colors repeated in the decor.

The guest parlour is filled with original and antique wicker furniture. Combined with an adjoining porch, guests are offered a quiet spot to relax within sight and sound of the Atlantic Ocean.

18

Joanne and Bob are truly at home with their guests and operate their inn with a relaxed and easygoing manner. Joanne described the atmosphere as being laid-back. "We leave our guests to themselves; people's vacations are their own—they come here to relax and enjoy." Homey and casual, seasoned guests have been known to sign themselves in, get their keys and go right on up to their room!

In common with the Holly House and the rest of the "Sisters" in between, the Myers' home has a spectacular curved staircase that joins the three floors. The building also faces away from Jackson Street and overlooks a private lane, Atlantic Terrace. Upon arrival, guests may pull around to the "front" and unload their luggage.

In the spring, Bob and Joanne devote hours to gardening in the flower beds surrounding their home. The rear walkway on Jackson Street has a spectacular springtime array of tulips, daffodils and lilies, which most certainly inspire some of Joanne's unique paintings. Every nuance of warmer weather brings more flowers of every variety to bloom throughout the summer. A low bench set along the edge of the brick walkway makes a perfect spot for contemplation. Guests are invited to use the spacious side lawn for sunbathing and exercising.

THE SEVENTH SISTER GUESTHOUSE, 10 Jackson Street, Cape May, N.J. 08240, (609) 884-2280. Bob and Joanne Myers, Innkeepers. One of the identical "Seven Sister" Houses designed by architect Stephen D. Button and individually listed on the National Register of Historic Places. Six rooms open to guests year 'round. Well-behaved children over 7 allowed. Indoor shower and luggage storage, which guests may use on day of check-out. Guest refrigerator. Nice touches: Bright and beautiful summer atmosphere year 'round—100 feet from beach, with sunporch facing ocean; original coal-grate fireplace in parlour to warm winter guests, art-gallery atmosphere.

The Gingerbread House

rim and white with green shutters and a jaunty striped
awning, the Gingerbread House is one of the famed eight
Stockton row-houses which were originally built in 1869
as summer rental cottages. The Stockton Cottages were
part of the 2,000 room Stockton Hotel estate which covered all of
the property several city blocks deep, running on the opposite side
of the street from the cottages, to the ocean. The "cottages" were
named as such because they were run by only three servants;
"villas" had a staff of seven and "mansions" commanded a staff of
ten! Neither by Victorian standards or today's, the Stockton
rowhouses were by no means bargain rentals—one summer season
in the 1870's cost a whopping $2,000!

Fred and Joan Echevarria, the young couple who own and operate
the Gingerbread House today, offer their home to guests year
'round. Upon entering the inn, you immediately feel a home-away-
from-home atmosphere, mainly brought on by the friendly nature of
the owners. Fred is an ex-clinical psychologist and presently
manages their guest house during the week, while Joan travels to
Philadelphia each day to manage the data-processing department for
a stock brokerage firm.

Relatively new to the "guesthouse phenomena", Fred and Joan
bought and opened their home by Memorial weekend 1980,
admittedly with a generous amount of help from family. The
Echevarrias gained much of their expertise in running a guest house
by staying and helping out at the Seventh Sister, which is owned and
operated by Fred's sister, Joanne Echevarria Myers and her
husband, Bob.

Guest rooms at the Gingerbread House are located on the second and third floors and are furnished with refreshingly simple oak and wicker furniture, hanging plants and some of Joan's needlework. Each floor shares a roomy bath, complete with brass lighting fixtures, pedestal sink and enormous tub. The halls and staircases are lined with some of Fred's best photographs, each enclosed in his handmade frames. The innkeeper's talents in woodworking are evident in the magnificent glass-paneled oak exterior doors, as well as in the downstair front parlour where a wonderful showcase coffee table and a showbox shelf feature Joan's shell collection. This room also has two lovely paintings, both given to the innkeepers by grateful guests.

Interestingly enough, the Gingerbread House is the only one of the eight Stockton cottages to contain a fireplace, and winter guests are invited in to relax and enjoy its warmth. Summer visitors can make use of a picture-perfect front porch, with its shaded awnings, hanging baskets of plants and wicker furniture.

When asked about the trim for which the Gingerbread House is named, the Echevarrias revealed that their first concern was to make the interior of their home comfortable for themselves and their guests. Foundational repairs are often made at the expense of exterior renovations; the job of restoring properties to Victorian splendor is slow and costly. Pieces of the original gingerbread have been found under their porch and eventually will be used as a pattern for new trim. In naming their home the Gingerbread House, Fred and Joan reveal a true commitment to the restoration of one of Cape May's own.

THE GINGERBREAD HOUSE, 28 Gurney Street, Cape May, N.J. 08204; (609) 884-0211. Fred and Joan Echevarria, Innkeepers. One of the Stockton Cottage Rowhouses built by architect Stephen D. Button and individually listed on the National Register of Historic Places. Six rooms open to guests year 'round. Master bedroom with private bath, two double beds and private porch. Continental breakfast and beach tags included. Well-behaved children over 5 allowed. Outside shower. Nice touches: Lots of personal artwork and fine carpentry; lovely front porch—very casual atmosphere and near to beach.

 Captain Mey's Inn

 his sturdy and massive home, high above Ocean Street, was the realization of a longtime dream for Innkeepers Carin Feddermann and Milly LaCanfora.

Built at the turn of the century, the more modern-looking exterior reflects the late Victorian reaction against the fanciful gingerbread trim. When the present owners stripped away forty years of rooming house furniture, makeshift kitchens and layers of paint, a most charming interior was revealed, with a central staircase, large Victorian parlour and dining room, guest rooms and solid oak woodwork throughout.

Just one step into the vestibule gives the visitor a taste of the extensive detail artists and craftsmen lavished on the interiors of Victorian homes. The foyer alone has three exquisite Tiffany stained glass windows set in oak, with a seashell design that is repeated in the ceramic wall tiles below.

Carin and Milly give their guests a "come on in and join the family" kind of greeting and their warm and homey atmosphere is carried throughout the house in decor and genuine European hospitality. The fact that Carin was originally from Holland inspired the two women to call their guesthouse Captain Mey's Inn, after another Dutchman—Cornelius Jacobsen Mey, who explored the New Jersey coast and gave Cape May its name.

The European touches are everywhere: a family heirloom collection of Blue Delftware, "portrait rooms" named in memory of family members, wall and over-the-bannister hung rugs and tapestries, including the most lovely lace curtains from Holland. The dining room fireplace, which was hidden behind a wall for 50 years, has recently been reopened, uncovering a beautiful oak mantel with carved lion heads and imported Delft-blue tiles. A leisurely breakfast, served fireside and family-style in the oak-lined dining room, also reflects the European flair—imported cheeses, homebaked breads and cakes, juices and coffee. During the summer months, breakfast moves outside to a wicker-filled veranda.

The second and third floor bedrooms feature a quaint mixture of antiques, wicker, brass and country decor. An immense under-the-

eaves room on the third floor has been converted to a unique bath, housing some of Carin's personal selections from a previous antique business in town.

During the summer months, a two-room suite with private side entrance and porch, is relinquished by the innkeepers to help accommodate the larger number of guests.

The warmer weather brings guests out to enjoy the sea air and stepping out onto the front porch, guests can well imagine Ocean Street of the 1890's, when it was affectionately nicknamed "Doctors' Row". Captain Mey's Inn itself was built in 1890 for Dr. Robbins of Philadelphia. The charming antique store across the street was then McCray's Pharmacy.

Captain Cornelius Mey declared the climate of Cape May was "like that of Holland—as good as home." Guests of Captain Mey's Inn can do some exploring of the town on their own and return to relax in an atmosphere of small-town warmth and friendship—it's better than home!

CAPTAIN MEY'S INN, 202 Ocean Street, Cape May, N.J. 08204; (609) 884-7793; 884-9637. Carin Feddermann and Milly La Canfora, Innkeepers. A turn-of-the-century bed and breakfast inn with an European flair. Seven guestrooms open year round. Private first-floor suite available during summer months. Children not permitted. Rates include breakfast and beach passes. Off-street parking and outside shower. Nice touches: Newly painted exterior with unusual plum-colored accents; guests welcome in kitchen; women's antique hat collection and stained glass windows on 2nd floor landing.

Hanson House

very wealthy whaling Captain Walden built a "stalwart
and steady" home back in 1892. His love for the sea was
reflected in the style of his house, which dispensed away
with all delicate cutaway trim and spindly towers. This
house actually looks seaworthy. Climbing up the front stairs gives
one the feeling of coming aboard; the wide wraparound porch and
railing could very well be a ship's deck. And Vera and Alfred
Hanson, the present owners, love it that way.

Both the house and the Hanson's are steeped in history. Their
families have been vacationing in Cape May since 1772. Following
family traditions, both Vera and Alfred spent summers and made
trips to this town since their own childhoods. In 1970, the Hansons
purchased this home, retired there full-time several years ago, and
opened their door to guests.

Catering almost exclusively to regular guests and families that
have been returning to stay year after year, the Hanson House is a
charmer. One step inside and all those childhood memories of going
over to grandmother's come rushing back. Vera Hanson, an
effervescent grandmother herself, calls their home a "potpourri of
yesteryear" and what a wonderful collection of things there are!

Tucked upon shelves, in china closets and upon the many pieces of antique furniture are collections of every kind,—commemorative plates, miniature tintype photographs, tiny paintings, spoons, tea cups and saucers, vases, nicknacks and bric-a-brac. Vera has personal collections of hats, old clothing and letters. There are pieces that go back to the 1700's—family heirlooms that they've lived with all their lives. As Alfred puts it, "We realized that there's too many things in the house; it could be thinned out, but there's nothing we can part with!"

In the lovely peach colored parlour, there are two impressive museum quality portraits of family ancestors, and both Vera and Alfred would be glad to fill in the family history of these and other items of interest around the house.

The front hall of the Hanson House is especially lovely with a stained glass window with a rose design, window seat and antique desk. Vera adds, "When a rose is present, that means the Queen has visited . . ." A small staircase leads to the second floor where four bright and comfortable guestrooms with a somewhat French Provincial feel to them are located. The halls and rooms are all luxuriously carpeted and Vera has even topped some rooms off with antique oriental area rugs. One room has a private bath, the other three each have their own washstand and share a beautiful bathroom, with a large porcelain pedestal sink and tub with shower. Vera has placed many lovely antiques for guests to admire throughout the house, and the bathroom is no exception.

During the summer months, the large dining room with a ship's style mantlepiece is converted into a private suite with three beds, private bath and private entrance from the porch.

A most noteworthy detail about this guesthouse is the exquisitely painted woodwork and doors. Captain Walden spared no expense with the thick wood trim and heavy molded doors and the fruits of Alfred Hanson's labors have likened the woodwork to something resembling creamed silk.

Alfred's talents also extend into the kitchen, where he takes over to prepare a tasty breakfast for his guests. During the year, his menu may include ham and eggs, seasonal fruits, cinnamon bread, local beach plum jelly and perhaps some fresh fish caught by one of his friends. Summer breakfasts are served outdoors, "on deck" where guests can sip tea in a rocker and watch ocean breezes ruffle the hanging greenery and a proud American flag.

THE HANSON HOUSE, 111 Ocean Street, Cape May, N.J. 08204; (609) 884-8791. Alfred and Vera Hanson, Innkeepers. A late 19th Century Inn with 4 guestrooms and one additional guest suite during summer season. Three guestrooms share bath. Rates include breakfast and beach passes. Open all year. Well behaved children permitted. Nice touches: Electric blankets in winter, monogrammed towels, backyard with picnic table and hibachi for summer guests.

The Queen Victoria

 ne of the most distinctive transformations a Victorian mansion has gone through in Cape May is at the corner of Ocean and Columbia Avenue, in the completely restored 1881-82 Douglas Gregory House.

For years it blended in with the neighboring houses—a row of Victorian "wedding cakes" whose dramatic architectural details were minimized by the traditional white paint.

Today, the Douglas Gregory House is known as The Queen Victoria, renamed by its new owners, Dane and Joan Wells. Committing themselves to a total renovation for their new home and country inn, they've even duplicated the original color placement for every architectural detail of its recent paint job.

The innkeepers are not new to the restoration process. Joan is the former director of the Victorian Society in America and was the curator of the Molly Brown House in Denver, Colorado. At the Victorian Society, she ran old house workshops all over the country, in conjunction with the Society's Old House Journal publication. In Denver, she designed and instituted the $400,000 restoration project at the Molly Brown House Museum. Dane, who admits a love for "tinkering around old houses and hardware

stores," brings to his inn a background of management in commercial revitalization programs; in and out of retailing for 20 years, he's organized community business associations and merchants to do physical improvements and renovations.

At one point in their lives, the Wells tried to purchase one of the three most spectacular properties in northern California to develop into an inn. The project was abandoned when they couldn't get a variance of the state's zoning law enabling them to transform a former town hospital into a country inn.

Hanging on to the idea of combining their expertise in consumer service and old house restoration, Dane and Joan continued a search for another property that took them through six states. They also consulted with Norman Simpson, "The Berkshire Traveler" and author of the well-known guide books, "Country Inns and Back Roads." Their travels, while looking for that special building, inevitably took them to Cape May, *the* town for old houses. It was here, with the help of Tom Carroll, innkeeper of the Mainstay and a primary advisor to many of the new innkeepers in town, that the Wells found their Victorian Queen.

Their first and largest undertaking in the renovation of the Gregory House was the painting of its exterior. In a stroke of genius, Dane persuaded the Sherwin Williams Company to give him 90 gallons of green and maroon paint in return for using The Queen Victoria in paint promotions for a new line of Victorian colors.

All throughout the winter of 1981, visitors, who came to get a peek at the activity going on inside the new inn in town, could catch a glimpse of Dane and Joan forever up on ladders and covered with dust as they cleaned, scraped, plastered, painted and wallpapered their way through 20 gallons of bleach, 300 lbs. of spackle, 20 gallons of paint and 203 rolls of wallpaper!

Their ambitious restoration plan took some 6500 hours of manual labor and the results are smashing. The thirteen guestrooms, with rich and vibrant color schemes based on the antique-reproduction wallpapers, are marvelous—patterns of deep brick red, olive greens, indigo blue and caramel browns. Rooms are named after famous British personalities—a side-by-side trio, amusingly labeled The Prince of Wales, Oscar Wilde and Lily Langtry, indicate the Wells fondness for BBC productions! Each room is meticulously decorated with their personality namesake in mind. The Charles Dickens room is covered with wallpaper that looks like the marblized endpapers of Victorian novels and an etching of the "Old Curiosity Shop" hangs on the wall. The Lily Langtry room, in periwinkle blue and pink has a bedcover and wallpaper sprinkled with lilies of the valley and sports a dramatic photo of its namesake.

The rest of the rooms are similarly decorated with antique bedspreads, colorful patchwork quilts (some handmade by Mennonite churchwomen from Lancaster, Pennsylvania), marble-topped dressers and carved rockers. Some of the larger rooms have sitting or reading areas with arm chairs and small tables.

On the main floor, all traces of 1950 renovations were removed, including a "modern" kitchen, picture windows and paneling. A long hall on the main floor was eliminated to allow for the enlargement of the dining room to its original dimensions.

Today's dining room provides an elegant setting for houseguests to help themselves to a homemade buffet-style breakfast consisting of fresh-from-the-oven bread, egg casserole, fresh fruit and juice, imported tea and coffee. Adjoining the dining area is a canopied side-porch filled with wooden rocking chairs, plants and a porch swing. Guests can easily move their morning meal out-of-doors when the weather permits.

    The most unique room at the Queen Victoria is the front parlour which is furnished with Dane and Joan's personal collection of Arts & Crafts "Mission" furniture. The solid oak pieces, characterized by their squarish, straight-backed style, often with leather seats and table tops, were popular from 1900 to 1920. A nice grouping in front of the massive brick fireplace and an interesting selection of reading material, make the parlour a natural spot for reading and socializing. An original Roycroft cabinet is filled with a lovely collection of Rockwood Pottery in shades of blue and plum.

The innkeepers relate that perhaps the most enjoyable time to stay at The Queen Victoria is when the summertime crowds have gone and Victorian lovers and sea-side strollers have the town to themselves. Christmas season is especially festive with special events planned for winter guests. During the holiday season, visitors can sign up for a three-day Christmas workshop on the art of decorating a Victorian house and a session on the "Victorian Christmas Dinner", giving advice on menus and recipes.

The emphasis here at The Queen Victoria is on providing guests with the simple, old-fashioned atmosphere of a 19th century country inn with many of the special services of a first-rate 20th century hotel.

THE QUEEN VICTORIA, 102 Ocean Street, Cape May, New Jersey 08204; (609) 884-8702; Dane and Joan Wells, Innkeepers. A thirteen room bed and breakfast inn, restored to Victorian elegance in celebration of the building's 1981 centennial. One block from ocean. Private and shared baths. Each room has a private sink. Open to guests year 'round. Country breakfast included. Suites of rooms suitable for families are available. Small refrigerator for guests' use. Nice touches: Special services for guests' convenience, such as steam iron and ironing board, sewing kits, shoeshine kits, alarm clocks, extra toiletries in bath. For quiet entertainment, books, toys, games and bicycles are provided.

Humphrey Hughes House

 ughes, a name long associated with Cape May's historical past, reappeared in 1981 as the "new boy in town." The Humphrey Hughes House brought the family name into an opulent present and a most promising future.

A fascinating history begins with Captain Humphrey Hughes, who sailed to Cape May in 1660. He was one of the original landowners of Cape May. Humphrey Hughes II purchased an additional tract of land known as Five-Mile Beach—here is the spot where today's Hughes House stands. Ellis Hughes, Cape May's first postmaster, maintained one of the two original public houses on Cape Island. The earliest known newspaper advertisement for a Cape May boarding house appeared in the Philadelphia Aurora in July 1801 and is credited to Ellis Hughes. A portion of its quaint and delightful description reads:

Sea Shore Entertainment at Cape May

The public are respectfully informed that the Subscriber has prepared himself for entertaining company who use sea bathing, and he is accommodated with extensive house room, with Fish, Oysters, Crabs and good Liquors—care will be taken of gentlemen's horses........

This was a time when gentlemen made the long journey to the Cape by carriage, stagecoach or packet boat.

In 1816, Thomas Hughes, Ellis' son, built the famous Congress Hall, then an unplastered, unpainted frame building, 3 stories high and 108 feet long.

The land on which the present-day Hughes House stands was long cultivated as farmland and was tilled right to the water's edge. In 1904, the property was sold to H. D. Justi (pioneer in the manufacture of porcelain teeth), who had the present home constructed by the York Brothers at a cost of $25,000. Dr. Franklin Hughes, who maintained a practice from what now is The Queen Victoria, purchased this house in 1925, and moved his doctor's office to the ground level of the home. From the late 20's, Dr. Harold Hughes (a descendant and one of Cape May's prominent physicians) and his family occupied the house, still in its original state with no renovations, until the doctor's death in July of 1980.

Today, this historically significant home is the vested interest of four prestigious businessmen who have added another restored and preserved guesthouse to Cape May's growing list.

The opulence of the Humphrey Hughes House can partly be attributed to the splendid interior and exterior condition of the building, with its elaborate brick front, columns and turned-wood railings. Miraculously, the ornately carved, solid chestnut walls, staircases and columns of the interior had never been painted. Interior designer Sandy Sheller got right to work with the exciting prospect of researching, restoring and redecorating the house in preparation for the soon-to-arrive guests.

Some of the original furniture and oriental rugs were Hughes' family pieces, some "goodies" were attic finds and more furnishings

were added from auctions and flea market trips. The designer paid particular attention to historically appropriate details and together with the museum quality furnishings, she has made the house a Victorian masterpiece.

The Humphrey Hughes House opened with five guestrooms on the second floor—each room, from the smallest West Wing of the Maid's Suite with its corner of framed memorabilia, to the grand Ocean View Room with its mirrored armoire and French mother-of-pearl inlay settee, is furnished most lavishly. Romantics will no doubt be tempted by the Red Velvet Room with floor-length velvet drapes, red satin comforter and a rare ruby glass Handel lamp trimmed with long black fringe. During the winter of 1982, four newly-renovated rooms were added on the third floor, featuring another ocean view room with a rose theme, the Brass Room, Grandmom's Nook and the Knave of Hearts Room. The interior charm of each, comes not only from the wonderful furnishings, but the imaginative color schemes and the small details worth noting: fresh flowers, designer and lace-trimmed sheets, plenty of small antiques to browse over, cross ventilation and delightful views of Cape May's mansard rooftops.

Both floors contain a handsome Victorian bath, each elaborately furnished with a claw-foot tub and shower, original brass fixtures, marble-topped sink and an authentic oak cabinet pull-chain toilet!

Coming downstairs, guests will pass Dr. Hughes' grandfather clock that sits on the staircase landing, keeping perfect time. The rest of the first floor, which includes the front hall entrance room, the parlour, dining room and another newly renovated "La Petit" guestroom, is well appointed with furnishings in the grand Victorian manner. The public is also welcome to take an informative first floor tour of the home which gives a good historical background of the family and the furnishings now present.

The promising future of the Humphrey Hughes House may well be in the hands of its innkeepers, carefully hired by the owners who cannot always be present. Filling this unique position to date, are Marge and Riley Holman—a warm and friendly (and recently married) couple who professionally spent their first season at The Humphrey Hughes House during the spring-summer-fall of 1982.

The *hired* innkeepers' job has created a homier atmosphere than expected in such opulent surroundings. Freed from the complex worries of a home-owner, the Holman's find they can devote themselves fully to their official job of pleasing "Ladies and Gentlemen on Seaside Holiday". To the delight of their guests, Marge and Riley have an easy sociability that includes spending time with their houseguests. Marge recalls, "One evening, there were twelve of us sitting around the fire, chatting till the wee hours of the night!"

The Humphrey Hughes House has successfully combined all the desirable attributes of an intimate guesthouse by the sea—historically impressive architecture, a rich and beautiful interior, a truly congenial atmosphere and all the amemnities that make an overnight stay memorable.

THE HUMPHREY HUGHES HOUSE, 29 Ocean Street, Cape May, N.J. 08204; (609) 884-4428; Marge and Riley Holman, Innkeepers. The original 1900 Hughes family home converted to a 10 room bed and breakfast inn, "For Ladies and Gentlemen on a Seaside Holiday." Two ocean view rooms and one first floor room with private bath, all other rooms share 3 additional baths. Open late March through mid-October. Home-prepared breakfast included. Nice touches: Large wrap-around veranda with view of ocean, screened-in sunporch, Italian game table in parlour. Full indoor private bath for guests' use, returning from beach, occasional live-music on the veranda.

The Abbey

 ay and Marianne Schatz, two of Cape May's most energetic and animated innkeepers, have made staying at The Abbey a real occasion. Guests are treated to a bed and breakfast inn that is a far cry from the plastic-filled, air-conditioned and a Color-TV-in-every room style of accommodation so prevalent today. The Schatzs have put together a unique combination of Victorian elegance within an atmosphere that is quite condusive to 20th century socializing.

For The Abbey's guests, the day begins with an elaborate continental breakfast surrounded by such treasures as a twelve foot solid mahogany dining table, East Lake chairs, an ornate gasolier and a massive sideboard made by a German cabinet-maker, who carved its three tiers with realistic animals, fish and fowl. Marianne relates, "Our breakfast is a way for guests to meet and enjoy each other. Guests wake up specifically early (8:30 a.m.) so as not to miss a thing—especially when Jay is serving, because he's a bit of an entertainer. Our early morning get-togethers are an icebreaker— after the second or third day, our guests are going out to dinner with each other!"

Aided by numerous old photographs and a lot of historical research (Marianne was a member of Cape May's Planning Board and both were involved with the restoration of the Physick Estate), the Schatzs have restored The Abbey to its former Victorian splendor. Guests, as well as the public, are invited to attend an entertaining first floor tour of The Abbey. Historical information about the architecture and the wealth of antique furnishings inside are amusingly embellished with bits of humor from both Marianne and Jay—whose head is usually topped for the occasion with an antique hat from his vast collection!

In 1869, John B. McCreary, a wealthy coal baron from Philadelphia, engaged Stephen D. Button (a well known architect of the period) to build an elegant summer villa for him in Cape May. Working a bit behind the times, Button designed a gothic revival structure at a time when many new buildings were of the Italianate style. The results were lovely nonetheless—stencilled and ruby-glass arched windows, front doors embellished with key-hole shaped moldings and rosettes, high ceilinged rooms with bay windows, shaded verandas, balconies and an impressive entranceway leading into the 60 foot church-like tower section of the building, which inspired its present name.

Inside, today's guests can linger in the past and marvel at the

faithful restoration and interior decoration that the Schatzs have devoted themselves to. A lavish first floor parlor is pure Victorian. The entire room is a myriad of browns—from the lightest ivory cream to deep chocolate, embellished with gold leaf. Floor-to-ceiling windows are hung with intricately pieced lambrekins of gold brocade that cleverly mirror the shape of the gothic arch. (Marianne reveals that her original design and production took some 80 hours to complete!) An exquisite hand-stenciled style wallpaper-border meets the molding, which trims the arched ceiling edge. As a popular ornamentation during Victorian times, the wallpaper borders are found in each and every room of The Abbey.

The parlour furnishings, including formal Victorian settees, side chairs and 15 foot mirrors, pay tribute to Clara Louise Kellogg, a 19th century opera star who began a trend in furniture making. Her famous face and shoulders, dressed in operatic garb, are carved into these and other furnishings of the period.

Oversized oriental rugs lead guests into the rear music corner, where an 1840 Swiss floor harp fills a window alcove. One can also plunk out a tune on a restored piano with a sound dated somewhere between harpsichord and baby grand!

The Schatzs have also solved the problem of illuminating the high-ceilinged rooms by amassing a wonderful collection of adjustable antique piano lamps. These elaborate lighting fixtures, with painted globes or romantic silk shades trimmed with long fringe, are tucked away in every conceivable corner.

Overnight guests of The Abbey climb a thick, ruby carpeted staircase to the second and third floor bedrooms situated off an interesting maze of hallways. Typically Victorian, all the "nooks and crannies" are filled with framed artwork, period pieces and momentoes from the 19th century.

The San Francisco Room, which was the original master bedroom of the house, is decorated in grand style with a tall, crested bed (featuring another carving of Miss Kellogg), topped with a satin comforter and matching pillows. Here one finds lace-drawn windows, a large armoire and a handmade tapestry bell-pull on the wall . . . a reminder of the days when it was connected to the servants' quarters below . . . Other guest rooms are equally charming with curly brass and iron beds, marble-topped dressers, dormered windows, wicker settees, electrified gas lighting fixtures and oriental rugs.

Most rooms have a private bath, but a real treat for those who must share, is the enormous bathroom in the tower. Here guests can enjoy a bird's eye view of Victorian rooftops and relax in a hot tub in a full-size room with stained glass windows, wall-to-wall carpeting and Victoriana decor.

Since 1977, The Abbey has been the pride and passion of the owners, who have taken great care in restoring their home with a true feeling of its original era. Specialists were hired to restore the roof as close as possible to the original red and grey patterned slate. Marianne nervously relates the story of the iron welder who came on the coldest and windiest day of winter to install the wrought iron cresting along the roof line! Their most recent project is the replacement of the original design picket fence which edged the property in its early days. With restoration plans that never seem to end, the Schatz-fantasy-for-the-future is the reconstruction of a whimsical gazebo that used to exist on their side lawn.

For thirty-four years, while the McCreary house was being used as a Christian Science Reading Room, it was painted completely white with its exquisite architectural details almost invisible. Inspired by the variety of shades in the original black and white photos of the house, the Schatzs were one of the first to take the plunge and paint their home in Victorian colors—finally deciding on light green, deep red and ivory. Perfection! The dazzling array of bric-a-brac, the seaside wavy clapboard shingles and beautiful gothic molding surrounding the windows and doors, at long last received a prominence they so well deserved! Jay's comment on the enormous project was that the next time they decide to paint, he'd paste up dollar bills on the house instead—that way they'd spend less money and still have the same color scheme!

THE ABBEY, Columbia Avenue and Gurney Street, Cape May, N.J. 08204; (609) 884-4506. Jay and Marianne Schatz, Innkeepers. A Gothic style villa recorded by the Historic American Buildings Survey for the Library of Congress. Open to guests from April to November. Rates include continental or full breakfast, afternoon refreshments and beach passes. Children and pets not permitted. Offstreet parking for guests. Mini-refrigerators in most rooms. Nice touches: After breakfast, the sights of Cape May from the top of the Abbey's 60 foot tower, occasional impromptu "happy hour" for guests returning from the beach, wine served during the House Tour.

The Duke Of Windsor

ne summer day, Fran Prichard answered the bell at her front door. A woman introducing herself as Helen York Shields, remarked, *"I've just come by to see the house my father built!"* Mrs. Shields, 92, was the daughter of one of the York Brothers who had designed and built this classic, grand-scaled home circa 1896.

During her stay, this most welcome visitor revealed many interesting facts to Bruce and Fran Prichard about their new bed and breakfast inn named in honor of England's fabled monarch, the Duke of Windsor. Sitting in the family parlour, the elderly woman recalled the days when she and her sister played on the floor using wood shavings as hair curls, while their father and his brothers worked at mounting the gas lights on the staircase baluster and installing the stained glass windows in the stairwell.

The house was being built for Mr. & Mrs. Harry Hazelhurst; Mrs. Shields remembered them as being very large people, who insisted on the generous dimensions of the rooms and the staircase!

Mr. Hazelhurst was a Delaware River boat pilot, as were many of his neighbors on Washington Street in the late 1890's. Helen Shields vividly described the sights and sounds of the "taxi-man" who came down the street with a horse and buggy to escort the pilots back and forth to the Delaware. With a megaphone, he'd yell out, "She's a'comin'!" All the men, including Mr. Hazelhurst, would rush out with their bags and hop on the buggy for the trip down to the river. Like any other innkeepers in town, the Prichards were *delighted* with the chance to learn some firsthand personal history of their new home and one of Cape May's newest bed and breakfast inns.

The Prichards explain that their interest in the guesthouse phenomena may have begun when longtime friends of theirs moved away to Cape May to open a bed and breakfast inn. Missing their company, while inspired by their success and new life-style, Fran and Bruce decided to begin looking for a guesthouse themselves. After an exhaustive search, the Prichards ultimately met their needs in terms of a private residence and a potential inn at 817 Washington Street.

Having to look past (and physically step over) tons of debris, furniture and clothes that lay strewn about a home which had remained unoccupied for years, the Prichards saw the obvious: a magnificent foyer with original woodwork and paneled wain-scotting, a carved oak open staircase that vaulted three stories, classic corner fireplaces with inset tiles and hand carved mantel-pieces, as well as ceilings superbly constructed with ornate plaster medallions and ribbons. This was certainly it! The perfect house—and it became the Prichard's own, late in the winter of 1982.

Guests of the new Duke of Windsor will enjoy the grand scale and turn-of-the-century character of the house. Many of the nine, highly individual guestrooms are of the large salon-type, furnished with period pieces specifically chosen for their charm and antique value. Sleeping areas are generous and some have additional sections for sitting, provided with comfortable armchairs and small tables. Polished hardwood floors are covered with antique oriental rugs, and windows are hung with imported English lace curtains. The high ceilings and numerous window exposures add to the spacious feel of each room—even the smaller ones, such as the two popular guestrooms in the forty-five foot tower section of the house.

On the main floor, guests can entertain themselves in the first floor tower room which has been transformed into a small game and conversation area. The decor of the large family parlour eclectically reminisces with different eras. Fran adds, "Along with comfort, we would like our guests to go back in time—whether it be the 1890's or the 1930's, it's still a nice trip!"

A most important feature of the bed and breakfast inn is the dining room. Here at the Duke of Windsor, an informal morning meal is staggered between 9 and 10 a.m. Guests can meet and greet each other over a generous dining room table, where a continental breakfast of cereal, fresh fruits, homemade breakfast cakes or muffins, and coffee and tea is served. Conversation is lively, with the typical exchanges of family and work backgrounds, travel experiences, or where the best place in town is for dinner. The surroundings are exceptional. Above the table, the entire ceiling is crisscrossed with elaborate curved moldings. The walls are wainscotted with "Lincrusta", a rare, deeply embossed wallcovering popular during Victorian times. A plate rail above, surrounds the room with a collection of colorful platters. Three large bay windows, with a window seat below, fill in the full west wall of the room.

The atmosphere at The Duke of Windsor is warm and friendly, as the Prichards thoughtfully put themselves in the shoes of the guests in anticipation of their needs. Having a wonderful house to start off with, Bruce and Fran have established a handsome bed and breakfast inn with a relaxed personality, much like their own!

THE DUKE OF WINDSOR, 817 Washington Street, Cape May, N.J. 08204; (609) 884-1355. Bruce and Fran Prichard, Innkeepers. A classic, Queen Anne style bed and breakfast inn, offering nine guestrooms, some with private baths. Open to guests from April 1 to October 30. Lodgings include continental breakfast, afternoon tea and beach badges. Enclosed outdoor showers and bicycle storage. Off the street parking provided. Children over 12 permitted. Nice touches: Large veranda furnished with pillow-covered settees; a wealth of elegant interior details in a casual atmosphere, and innkeepers who enjoy spending time with guests.

The Victorian Rose

he Victorian Rose is a relatively new guesthouse, having "blossomed" in the spring of 1981 under the ownership of a young couple who combined their experiences in restoring old furniture and restoring old houses. Bob Mullock, with a career in marketing communications and Linda Mullock, a former Montessori schoolteacher, successfully jumped right into the sensitive job of owning and operating a guesthouse.

The Mullocks relate some personal views: "We feel this is a great location, and a kind of cornerstone in Cape May—being two doors down from the Chalfonte and four homes away from the Mainstay. We like to think of Howard Street as our house-lined driveway to the beach. Our guesthouse was built by the famous Stephen D. Button in 1872 and has an interesting history and the potential for a great romantic atmosphere. It has been a private summer residence, a public tea room, an all-girls' school and a guesthouse, formerly well known as the Southern Inn."

After months of renovations, the Mullock have put together a charming new inn that touches on Victorian, but includes the best of other eras. Glen Miller and early Frank Sinatra tunes play in the parlour. Lots of new antique-collectables are tucked here and there:

framed Wallace Nutting potographs, Betsy Pease Gutman prints, a calendar, family photos and pink depression glassware.

After removing a wall that ran the entire length of the front hallway, the main entrance now opens into a large columned parlour with a salon atmosphere. The original floor has been sanded and polished. A romantic color scheme of pinks, greens and black appears in the area rug, a tapestry print carved settee, framed portraits, vases of fresh roses and potted palms. The only victorian "stuffiness" in this room is the velvet overstuffed chair in the corner sitting under a silk fringed reading lamp. Bob and Linda want their guests to feel casual and not intimidated by furnishings—which are there for each guest's enjoyment.

The Victorian Rose offers a variety of accommodations. There are eight guest rooms furnished with carved beds, marble-topped

dressers and newly purchased antiques. Room one, a favorite with honeymooners, and the only guestroom on the first floor, has floor-to-ceiling windows that open onto the veranda. If you don't mind hearing some porch conversations while in your room, this one has a private bath and no stair climbing. The room features a very special Victorian bed previously shown in the Cape May County Museum and the Physick Estate. The innkeepers will fill in the interesting details of this auction purchase for the Victorian Rose.

The second floor rooms open onto a long sun-filled hallway. Each

room retains its original screen door, which allows the interior door to be left open as guests can fill their rooms with cross-breezes from the ocean.

Guestrooms on the third floor are furnished with iron beds the Mullocks purchased from a hotel in Paradise Park, Pennsylvania, a popular resort in the Gay Nineties. A small reading room fills the space between these two rooms and offers a quiet retreat with a birds'-eye view of the ocean. A tiny electric candle has been burning in its window for ten years. "People come and tell us when our light burns out. Fishermen can see it from the ocean as they sail by. We feel it's a nice romantic tradition, especially appropriate here in Cape May," reflects Linda.

The bed and breakfast theme seems to stimulate guests to socialize with each other, knowing all will be sharing the same breakfast table. A sunny morning and the smell of the day's first meal bring guests out to the porch to wait for the call. On the veranda, there are plenty of high-backed wooden rockers, small tables, hanging plants and a chance to greet and meet other guests. The afternoon and evening is usually private and tip-toe quiet, so it's a pleasant surprise to see sixteen or so guests appear for breakfast!

Originally part of a public tea room, the dining room at the

Victorian Rose retains much of the flavor from that era. An impressive 8-foot tall sideboard and matching server with turned columns, beveled mirrors and carved doors was acquired from the Boardman Estate (Boardman was the designer of the famous boardwalk of Atlantic City, N.J.). High-backed oak chairs surrounding an exquisitely carved oak pedestal table, easily accommodate a houseful of guests.

Linda whimsically sets the table with her collection of antique cups, saucers and plates. Each guest enjoys a different floral design, many in keeping with the Victorian rose motif spread throughout the house. The continental breakfast is refreshingly light and may include orange juice, plenty of coffee or tea, bowls of fresh summer fruit salad served in stemmed glasses, homemade walnut and raisin-cinnamon buns or cheese-onion quiche.

The Victorian Rose is one of Cape May's newer inns that has gracefully matured with each continued improvement. It has been fun to watch all their plans for the future truly happen. The proposed rose garden now has 100 new plantings. The charming exterior of the house has been transformed by shades of blue and rose, and the interior upgraded with many historical antiques. No doubt, guests' opinions will always be valued as the Mullocks share their enthusiasm and plans to make the Victorian Rose even *more* special!

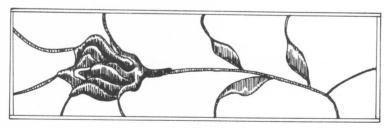

THE VICTORIAN ROSE, 715 Columbia Avenue, Cape May, N.J. 08204; (609) 884-2497; Robert and Linda Mullock, Innkeepers. An 1872 Bed and Breakfast Inn with eight guestrooms, some with private baths. Additional rentals include apartments with kitchen and private bath and a separate cottage known as the "Innlett", which sleeps five and has a full kitchen. Open to guests year round. Families with children are welcome in the Innlett cottage and apartments. Guest refrigerator located on second floor. Beach passes available. Outdoor shower. Nice touches: Very casual, no "rules of the house" tacked behind each door; small complimentary bottle of wine and two glasses greet each guestcouple. Holiday Specials available.

 The Brass Bed

 he disappearance of the quiet, uncluttered Philadelphia suburbs was the underlying reason for the Dunwoody family's search for a new living environment. With two school-age children at home to raise, John and Donna longed to return to a safe, small-town atmosphere. John's background in restoring and renovating old buildings in the Haddonfield, New Jersey area and Donna's intrigue with the guesthouse business ultimately led them to Cape May. The town held what they were looking for—old houses by the sea, tree-lined streets, quiet nights and friendly neighbors.

After much research, they found a house in the heart of the historical district that would provide ample living quarters for the owners and plenty of rooms to share with guests. Their large and graceful home, built in the early 1870's, is of the gothic revival style. A wide columned porch shaded by sycamore trees fills the front yard.

Renovated during the winter of 1980 with the help of two of their three children, the Dunwoodys opened their doors on Memorial Day, 1980. Naming their inn The Brass Bed for nostalgia's sake, the owners soon found out that their earliest guests expected to find brass beds throughout. Today's guests do: all guestrooms are furnished with Victorian brass beauties, combined with family pieces and original wooden furniture of the house. An especially lovely room on the second floor overlooks historic Columbia Avenue. The subject of a prize-winning photograph, it features a polished brass bed sitting in a windowed corner under yards of billowey organdy curtains. A large walnut wardrobe, oak dresser and tables and an oriental rug complete a *most* romantic scene.

Although most of the house has been stripped, plastered, painted and papered, it retains an uncanny feel of a century past. John and Donna make a concerted effort to keep their guesthouse filled with touchable "good old things" in a family-home atmosphere. John adds, "Our goal is to create an atmosphere like one might recall during a visit to grandma's house. Breakfast is a great time to be with our guests—we've met so many interesting people and shared many wonderful stories with them." The morning meal is served in the front dining room under the watchful eye of John's great-grandparents, who appear in two 1878 framed photographs on the wall. Guests will be amazed at the startling resemblance John has to his great-grandfather! An old-fashioned gasolier (gas and electric chandelier) hangs over the large table where the innkeepers serve a breakfast of juice, fresh baked goods, coffee, tea and cereals, while sharing lively conversations with their guests.

Across the hallway, in a parlour with floor-to-ceiling windows, is a collection of furnishings straight from grandmother's attic: a platform rocker, a Victorian settee, a marble-topped rosewood table, a 1905 Smith Corona typewriter sitting on an 1850 desk, and even a Grafonola (a windup phonograph), complete with a selection of old records.

Most guesthouse owners like to do a little research on the history of their home to provide what John quips, "a little historical schmaltz to give some character to the house", and to give answer to the many inquiries from the guests. John's delving into the past revealed their home to be included in several old photographs and illustrations showing the row of houses on Columbia Avenue that were built and privately owned by prestigious members of Philadelphian society. The Dannenbaum family was the first owner and retained the house for fifty-eight years. In 1930, Dr. Alexander Arthur, a prominent Philadelphian physician who was rumored to be the nephew of President Chester A. Arthur, purchased the house. It is known that President Arthur did stay in Cape May and the Dunwoody's curiosity has been peaked as to a possible connection to their home. The Dunwoodys made their purchase from the children of Mary Rogers, who, as a ward of the Arthurs, had been willed the house when Mrs. Arthur died. For fifty years, the home was known as the The Woodbine Guest House. The Arthurs also owned another guesthouse on Franklin Street named The Wisteria and together these were called The Flower Cottages. Even to this day, the Dunwoodys are hosts to occasional guests who originally stayed with the Arthurs at The Woodbine and recall Dr. Arthur as quite an eccentric character!

Both John and Donna are now full-time innkeepers. John no longer commutes to an advertising position in Philadelphia. He recalls, "I was going crazy getting to my job while Donna stayed home and had all the fun!" From the very beginning, the Dunwoodys liked the idea of the extended season in Cape May and they keep their welcome sign up all year. During the late fall, things begin to slow down a bit, but guests who enjoy being treated like friends keep coming by for those winter get-away weekends at The Brass Bed.

THE BRASS BED, 719 Columbia Avenue, Cape May, N.J. 08204, (609) 884-8075. John and Donna Dunwoody, Innkeepers. A 112 year old Gothic revival Victorian guesthouse on historic Columbia Avenue. Open to guests year round. Rates include full breakfast and beach passes. Eight guestrooms, suites available. Children over 12 permitted, no pets. Large 1930's refrigerator on second floor hallway for guests' use. Nice touches: Lovely exterior paint job in Victorian colors, shaded veranda with wood and rush rockers, most hospitable and accommodating innkeepers.

The Barnard-Good House

n the west side of Cape May's busy historic district, the Barnard-Good House stands, looking like an Edward Hopper canvas just waiting to be painted. Built on property that was once part of the Congress Hall estate, this three-story 1868 cottage is a gingerbread dream, with layers of lacy frosting; from the bric-a-brac trimming the wraparound porch, to the woven cotton fantasies hanging in each window! The original picket fence surrounds the house and a storybook garden filled with climbing vines, and splashes of color provided by hydrangea, cosmos, marigolds, zinnias and geraniums. The family Irish Setter sitting on the side veranda fittingly completes the Victorian scene.

Owners Tom and Nancy Hawkins fondly recall meeting this delightful cottage several years ago on a getaway trip of their own. Unhappy with their careers and commuting, in addition to an "empty family nest", the Hawkins were ripe for a change. The idea of running a guest house was born after a stay at Mrs. Baldt's Cottage on Gurney Street. Nancy recalls the return trip home— "During the 100 miles up the coast of New Jersey, we discussed

every reason why we would be good at this guesthouse business." The planning began immediately and soon the Hawkins found a perfect house. "It must have been right . . . we moved in and from that day on, we never once missed the house we lived in all those years." Nan added, "I feel more comfortable and happier here than I ever did."

Both workaholics, the Hawkins found running a guesthouse presented them with plenty of chores to keep them happy and busy. They live in the rear area of the house and like many of their innkeeping colleagues, do not employ any extra help. Tom has the daily routine of changing bed-linens and towels, while Nancy spends hours preparing menus and mouth-watering breakfast goodies for their guests. The rest of the time is devoted to renovating and maintaining their inn to a level of what Nan calls "understated elegance".

The lovely guestrooms on the second and third floors of the Barnard-Good House (named after their respective great-grand-parents) meet with that description. Antique-patterned paper covers the walls and rooms are furnished with family heirlooms and newly-purchased antiques. All windows are hung with long lace curtains trailing on the carpet like Victorian bridal veils. A front corner room features a graceful mahogany four poster bed with a pale gold canopy trimmed with fringe and tassels. Luckily, all woodwork throughout the house had never been painted and each southern pine door sports its original wooden doorknob!

Downstairs, guests can rest comfortably in a cozy front parlour where a variety of colors, textures and prints reflect the Victorian mode of pattern-on-pattern in a most charming way. Against one wall, there is an unusual mirrored and tiled fireplace, and opposite, a tiny antique carved organ just waiting to be played.

A new and unique addition to the Barnard-Good House is a completely renovated dining room with a "Turkish Corner". Nancy explains, "In the late 19th century, Victorians went wild for the lure and mystique of the Orient—they took odd corners of their homes and transformed them into exotic retreats. We decided this would be perfect for our dining room alcove—a real conversation piece!"

Breakfasts are Nancy's specialty and the luscious smells drifting upstairs summon guests to come on down for a real treat. She loves to "keep 'em guessing" by serving exotic combinations of freshly blended fruit or vegetable juices and hot-from-the-oven breads and

breakfast cakes with deliciously surprising ingredients. A typical
morning meal, served on a beautifully set table, might include
apple-carrot juice, piping hot homemade croissants, lettuce bread,
granola-peanut butter muffins with currant jelly and butter, herbal
teas and coffee. The breakfast conversation is as varied as its guests,
but with all the "mmm's" going on while eating, it naturally gets
around to Nan's cooking, exchanging recipes and talk about her
soon-to-be published breakfast cookbook!

With full stomachs, guests usually continue their conversation
on one of the loveliest front porches in all of Cape May. Sitting in
white wicker rocking chairs amidst cascading ferns and geraniums,
with a backdrop of lace and shuttered windows and layers of
gingerbread trim all around, guests can well imagine themselves

right in the middle of a Victorian picture postcard. Tom informs September guests to watch for hordes of Monarch butterflies, which pass over and sometimes stop by the Hawkins' summer garden on their way to Mexico.

History recalls, many of the original guests came to Cape May by water and today's summer travelers can do the same. Since the Barnard-Good House is located on the original route leading into Cape May since steamboat days, the Hawkins have decided to revive an old courtesy that was extended to the earliest guests arriving in Cape May. Today's visitors coming by ferry from Lewes, Delaware for a stay at the Barnard-Good House can leave their cars on the Delaware side. The Hawkins will pick up guests once they reach Cape May Point and bring them right to the door. All historic sights and the beach are within walking distance, and true to the nineteenth-century feel of the town, cars are delightfully unnecessary.

Warm and friendly by nature, Tom and Nancy take pride in getting to know their many guests and making sure they feel at home. The Hawkins' deep-rooted hospitality and enthusiasm as innkeepers are quite evident as they are quickly building up a regular clientele, as well as making many new and dear friends.

THE BARNARD-GOOD HOUSE, 238 Perry Street, Cape May, N.J. 08204; (609) 884-5381. Tom and Nancy Hawkins, Innkeepers. A Victorian Gingerbread home with 6 guestrooms. Open April to November. Four guestrooms on second floor share a powder room and full bath. Newly renovated third floor includes bath with Victorian copper tub, guestroom and a suite with private 2-piece bath. Rates include home-cooked continental breakfast and beach badges. Children over 12 permitted. Off-street parking. Full refrigerator for guests' use. Nice touches: wine glasses for guests' use, bicycles available to borrow and even a raincoat and umbrella for those who enjoy a spring shower!

The Mainstay Inn and The Cottage

he Mainstay . . . just the name conjurs up visions of an elegant plantation of the Gone With the Wind era: sweeping veranda, tall columns, summer evenings sipping mint juleps under trees dripping with Spanish moss . . .

The fantasy isn't so far-fetched. In 1872, a pair of wealthy Mississippi planters hired a famous architect to build a private clubhouse in fashionable Cape May, where their friends could gamble and engage in other "gentlemanly pleasures". No expense was spared in their grand Italianate villa. Tall, ornately carved pillars and brackets defined a wide veranda, which swept around three sides of the structure. A jaunty cupola topped the second story. The interior was pure luxury on a grand scale, with fourteen-foot ceilings, rich plaster moldings and ceiling medallions, elaborate wrought iron and brass chandeliers and a wide central staircase. Much of the furnishings were custom-built for the house and included twelve-foot, gilt and walnut mirrors and the finest ornamented furniture.

The Jackson Clubhouse is now over one hundred and ten years old, but it seems as if time has stood still for this Victorian structure. Passersby still stop and stare at the unexpected beauty of its exterior and grounds.

A young couple, Tom and Sue Carroll were also caught up in its beauty. The Carrolls came to Cape May when Tom was there on duty with the U.S. Coast Guard. They lived on Jackson Street in a turn-of-the century home which they owned and operated as a bed and breakfast guesthouse.

In 1971, the owners of the Jackson Clubhouse decided to sell. Known for years as "The Victorian Mansion", it was operated as a museum with guestrooms. As a result, the house was exceptionally well preserved with much of the original furnishings intact. It was also a beautiful piece of historical property, with all the potential for becoming a living testimony of Cape May's glorious past.

Needless to say, the Carrolls ended up purchasing the Victorian Mansion. Changing its name to The Mainstay Inn, they began the most exhausting but satisfying job of transforming their new home into a lavishly decorated country inn by the sea.

After much research into "appropriate Victorian interiors" and hundreds of hours of manual labor, Tom and Sue created a faithful restoration that easily transports one back to the 19th century. The hands-off museum areas which were the original gambling parlours are now delightful sitting rooms. Guests can relax in a room fit for Lily Langtry—with its stuffed chairs, globe lamps, grandfather clock, antique gambling table and cast-iron gas heater set in front of the fireplace. Sue's flair for decorating and handwork is particularly evident in the lambrekin window treatments and the hand-stenciled borders of these rooms.

The formal dining room is now the focus of hospitality, where in two seatings, 16 to 18 houseguests are served a hot breakfast, garnished with fruits, homemade cakes and breads. Overhead is the original cut-glass and brass chandelier which has been electrified for 20th century needs. Floor to ceiling windows, thick with Victorian lace, open onto the veranda where guests are served a continental morning meal during the warmer months.

A tradition at the Mainstay is afternoon tea. At four o'clock, guests eagerly return to the dining room for a cup, accompanied by some of Sue's homebaked goodies. On certain days, tea time follows an informative house tour given by either Tom or Sue. Both houseguests and interested visitors are invited to hear about the earliest days of the Jackson Clubhouse and all of its magnificent original furnishings and antiques. Afterwards, all may join in for refreshments. Sue reveals that many of their overnight guests plan their entire day around the afternoon tea!

Sleeping accommodations vary from cozy Country Victorian, to rooms more lavishly appointed. All are decorated with equal care in an authentic manner, using stenciled wood pieces, wrought iron beds, dark carved wooden headboards, tall wardrobes and framed period paintings and prints. Front rooms upstairs are named after famous Americans who have stayed in Cape May—Abraham Lincoln, Henry Clay and Ulysses S. Grant. The shared bathroom is enormous with a copper tub framed in wood and lots of living greenery.

For a lovely view of Cape May and the Atlantic Ocean clear down to the Delaware Bay, one can climb the narrow ladder on the second floor landing which leads to the rooftop cupola. The tiny glass enclosed room has been furnished with cheerful cushioned window-seats—a perfect solitary retreat!

Recently, the Carrolls purchased a 14-room house built in 1870, located next door to The Mainstay. Being a derelict property, Tom and Sue took on an extensive job of renovation which kept them busy all winter and well into the spring. Spacious new accommodations include five beautifully restored guestrooms, each with private modern baths and decorated with period wallpapers, globe lamps, tall carved headboards, Victorian furniture and antiques. This new addition has been affectionately named The Cottage. The two properties are joined by a flowered walkway and encircled with an extension of The Mainstay's lovely picket fence.

The most appealing spot for many guests is the wonderful veranda. Here is the place where one can linger in the past, resting on a thick-pillowed porch swing or in a wooden rocking chair. The grounds are spacious and well-tended. Flower beds of impatiens, tiger lilies, roses, petunias and hydrangea edge around the two houses and along the picket fence. Guests can also relax in a porch hammock or have a game of croquet on the lawn.

Tom and Sue Carroll have definite ideas about innkeeping and the atmosphere found here seems to reflect all the things they hold dear: "Converting our house into an inn has worked for us. It has placed us in the house of our dreams and surrounded us with wonderful people who share our enjoyment in restoration, antiques and old-fashioned comfort and friendship."

THE MAINSTAY INN and THE COTTAGE—635 Columbia Avenue, Cape May, N.J. 08204; (609) 884-8690, Tom and Sue Carroll, Innkeepers. A 9 room Italianate style villa with 5 additional guestrooms in an adjoining Victorian cottage. Open from April to November. Rates include breakfast and afternoon tea. There are 2 breakfast seatings; houseguests must make reservations. Private and shared baths. Small refrigerators available for guests' use. Nice touches: Museum quality furnishings and settings provided for guests' enjoyment; lots of antique periodicals and wealth of information on Cape May personally given by Tom or Sue.

RESTAURANTS

Alexander's

quiet elegancy describes the dining atmosphere of Alexander's, housed in a gray-blue Victorian structure with a scalloped wrought-iron fence edging its perimeter. Located in the heart of Cape May's business district, Alexander's has a rather interesting past.

It is timely to note that the house was built by a woman and was always owned by women until the late 1960's. Sara Leeming had the dwelling constructed in the early 1880's for her daughter, who in turn, left the house in a will to *her* two daughters, Jennifer and Sara. It is reputed that these two women were quite fanatical in preserving their home exactly as their mother had it. Never marrying, Jennifer and Sara lived together all their lives and until they passed away in 1963, their home virtually remained a Victorian time-capsule.

The women's reign of this property was over in 1967 when the city purchased the house for back taxes. Luckily, historical preservationists were springing up just about this time and when Cape May received its National Historical Landmark status, the building was narrowly saved from being razed. At some point the building was also titled the Joseph Hughes House after the husband of the original owner.

The tradition of naming a home after a family member is still alive today—the current young and amicable owners, Larry and Diane Muentz have named their restaurant and private residence after their son Alexander. Since purchasing the property in 1978, the Muentz's have taken the course of many other vintage homeowners in *personally* completing the major renovation jobs necessary to make a home-business livable and workable. Their 23 room mansion has been lovingly restored as a gracious restaurant and country inn, with the intense care usually reserved for a family dwelling. Fittingly, the earlier, strong presence of women in this house is revived in the tiny being of Diane Muentz, who at 5'2" and a size 3, tends to surprise guests as they learn she is the head chef in the kitchen. Right at home in the varied aspects of running a restaurant, Diane's background includes earning an interior design license at 19 and being a baker specializing in wedding cakes for 10 years before going to restaurant school in Philadelphia to learn the total trade.

Today, as Diane spends her time in the kitchen, Larry's domain is out front, where formally attired in black-tie, he greets guests and oversees the dining rooms personally, making sure customers are receiving top-notch service and enjoying a leisurely dinner to the fullest.

The fruits of the Mentz's talents are partially evident in Alexander's carefully decorated Victorian dining rooms filled with their refinished antique furniture, crystal chandeliers, period paintings and lacy handmade curtains at every window. Harpsichord music plays in the background. Their talents are further apparent when one tastes the savory creations coming out of the kitchen.

Diane shares a bit of her cooking philosophy which certainly has contributed to Alexander's success. Speaking softly, but with a mischievous twinkle of the eye, she explains her own little campaign against the exclusive American restaurant that requires the average customer to speak French to read the menu and order a meal. She believes this hypocrisy reached its peak during Victorian times when the great American chefs went to France to study, then returned to invent dishes in this country while giving them French names to assure international acceptance. At Alexander's, Diane has developed what she calls a "Private American Home Cuisine" whereby almost everything she serves is based on her own original recipes. Her most favorite time for cooking is before and after the summer season when the crowds are smaller, the menu is handwritten each day, and the gourmet dishes can change with a whim or on the availability of seasonal foodstuffs. She stays away from "classics" and frequently engages her well-educated, creative kitchen staff to help decide on a *special* specialty of the day. ("Once

77

we transformed three cases of very ripe bing cherries into the most exquisite chilled cherry and burgundy soup!")

During the height of their season, the popularity of certain dishes demands a traditionally printed menu so regular customers can find their favorites. Guests usually have a choice of 6 appetizers, eleven to twelve entrees, 4 desserts, plus additional entree and dessert specialties of the day. The food is strictly gourmet, individually prepared with strong American and occasional international flavor.

There are wonderful surprises at every turn—*none* of the predictable appetizers appear on the menu. Replacing the shrimp/fruit cocktail, clam-on-the-halfshell and tomato juice syndrome, are a creative selection of meal openers, including a rich sausage, nut, cream cheese and herb strudel; black caviar and sour cream with homemade melba toast; a mouth-watering cream of crab soup or a chilled platter of fresh, crisp vegetables and fruits with a spring dip.

To choose an entree is difficult—all favorites are included, from the freshest of fish to beef, veal and chicken dishes. Diane has worked magic on these basics, transforming them into adventures in taste. A cornish game hen is marinated and roasted with a soy-honey-plum glaze; chicken are breasts coated with ground pecans or sauteed with black and green olives and white wine. The prime steak arrives with a zingy Bernaise sauce and bubbled under the broiler; Steak au Poivre is a seductive dish with a spicy Espanole sauce flamed in cognac.

Tender jumbo shrimp in mango-chutney sauce comes to the table baked in a ring of cheddar-cheese puff pastry, while the most delicately prepared calves liver is sauteed in a wonderful compliment of onions, oranges and Sweet Dubonnet wine . . . and the list goes on and on.

Indulging in one of these exciting entrees whets one's appetite for a sure-to-be delectable dessert. Again it will be hard to choose: The New York Times billed Diane's frozen white chocolate Brandy Alexander Pie as "absolutely decadent." Diane relates the dessert is actually a drink you can eat with a fork and that it took her six weeks to figure out how to freeze all that alcohol! There's also semi-sweet chocolate fudge fondue with fresh fruits and goodies for dipping, a generous portion of hazelnut cheese cake, Brie cheese with white grapes, homemade ice cream of continually changing flavors—the licorice is tintillating!

Sundays at Alexander's is especially pleasant. A very elegant brunch is served from 9 to 1 with an elaborate menu including choices of fresh-ground coffees and imported teas, fresh fruits, appetizers, entrees and desserts which vary weekly. On Sunday evenings, after enjoying dinner or just dessert, Larry and Diane will personally guide guests through their home, pointing out the extensive restoration techniques used and explaining the Victorian life style splendidly recreated at Alexander's.

ALEXANDER'S, 653 Washington Street, Cape May, New Jersey 08204; (609) 884-2555. Larry and Diane Muentz, owners. A major renovation has taken place at Alexander's.—Their authentically restored 23 room mansion has been transformed into a full-service country inn featuring elegant dining and four new guestroom accommodations reflecting the Victorian life-style. Overnight guests are treated to breakfast in their guestrooms (morning meal only included in room rates). Rooms available April 1 to Thanksgiving. The Chandelier Room and Porch dining featuring Private American Home Cuisine; gourmet cooking 6 nights a week during summer (restaurant section closed Tuesdays). Open weekends in Spring to Memorial Day and Labor Day through Thanksgiving. Dinners served from 6 p.m. to 10 p.m. Sunday brunch from 9 a.m. to 1 p.m. No alcoholic beverages served: guests may bring their own at a service charge of 75¢ per person (ice bucket, corkscrew and wine glasses provided). Nice touches: After studying Ikebana for a year with a Japanese flower master, Diane expertly decorates Alexander's with elaborate fresh flower arrangements.

The Washington Inn

oby and Rona Craig originally came to Cape May to raise their children in South Jersey's small-town atmosphere. Toby had been involved with country club management and both were interested in the restaurant business. Several years ago, they bought the Washington Inn, which at that time had been a well-established restaurant and guesthouse for more than forty years. The inn is now the Craig's private residence, as well as a charming restaurant set amidst a large, landscaped corner on historic Washington Avenue. Before its transformation into a restaurant, this house had been privately owned for nearly a century.

The earliest photo of the 1846 house shows the original two-story columned front with a picket fence surrounding the property. In 1856, it was purchased by Thomas Quigg, who had the house moved away from the street to the rear corner of the lot. Quigg also did some remodeling, removed the columns and lowered the roof to create a second story porch. He also changed his mind about the position of the house and later had it placed on rollers and returned to its original spot where it still stands today! With all this moving around, it's a small wonder someone didn't chop down the rare Japanese Cryptomearia trees out front, but there they stand—

cousin to the redwood and 75 feet high. Toby exclaims that these trees are only one-half of their full height and have been growing in the front of the inn for one hundred years!

The popularity of the Washington Inn is growing by leaps and bounds. Summer crowds cause a bit of a wait to be seated, but on the front veranda, outfitted with thick-cushioned wicker sofas and rockers, patrons can rest and wait in comfort and enjoy the fresh air. For those who like a cocktail before dinner, they can step inside to a newly renovated room with a magnificent Victorian bar, designed and built by the owner from a French mirrored armoire, leaded glass window panels and solid wooden antique doors.

Kitchen and dining areas fill the entire first floor. The spacious dining rooms are decorated in what Rona calls "eclectic Early American". Walls are papered in a deep maroon floral print and tables covered with bright blue linen. There are framed works of art, tiny wall lamps and two working fireplaces to complete the scene for cozy dining.

The cooking staff at the Washington Inn specializes in a fine Americana menu well stocked with the traditional "by land" and "by sea" dishes. Purists, who favor a basic meat-and-potato meal without the fancy sauces, will savor such straightforward choices as N.Y. Strip Steak, lightly battered Veal Cutlets, Roasted Turkey with old fashioned stuffing, Colonial Fried Chicken and a tenderly marinated London Broil.

Local catches of the day bring in all the fresh fish needed to prepare a meal, such as Seafood Washington—a house specialty which is a delicious presentation of sauteed lump crabmeat, shrimp, open clams, mussels and lobster claws. All seafood entrees are today-fresh, delicately prepared, broiled for the most part and attractively presented. Again the seafood choices are standard fare—delicate crabmeat Stuffed Flounder dish; tender Ocean Scallops; broiled Butterfly Shrimp swimming in butter and garnished with fresh curly spinach; lump Sauteed Crabmeat and Lobster Tails.

Full dinner fare begins with a taste of sweet and sour sliced cucumbers, followed by a garden-fresh salad bowl of mushrooms, lettuce, spinach, radishes and juicy Jersey tomatoes. Try the tangy white French house dressing for a treat. Warm croissants and sweet rolls baked on the premises arrive neatly tucked in a little basket. A choice of potato and a good cup of coffee is included in the moderate price of a meal.

Desserts are of the homemade variety, and the selection changes with the fruit in season. Chocolate curls above and chocolate crust below surrounds a triple chocolate mousse. There are strawberries and cream, fruit cheesecakes and pies, and after dinner liqueur flavored ice creams.

An extensive wine list, including full bottles, carafes and half-carafes, is moderately priced.

The most popular spot to dine during the summer months is the lovely east wing of the veranda which has been outfitted for fresh air dining with screens, ceiling fans and hanging plants. A charming view includes a tiny Victorian flower garden, complete with bird-bath. Shrubs and century-old trees shade and make this a romantic private spot for dining.

The Craigs continue the good food tradition of the Washington Inn with many improvements and a few changes—they no longer accept overnight guests. Today's popularity of their restaurant business demands all their time and involvement. Truly a family affair, their children and close friends are employed with the regular staff to make things taste good and run smoothly.

THE WASHINGTON INN, 801 Washington Street, Cape May, N.J. 08204; (609) 884-5697; Rona and Toby Craig, Hosts. An 1846 early Victorian structure, housing a traditional-menu restaurant. Open weekends in March, April, October, November and December. Open 7 days a week from Memorial Day to the end of September. Dinners served from 5 pm. Earlybird specials are offered from 5 to 6 pm and House Specialties are available nightly. No reservations taken. Open all year to parties and/or catered affairs and weddings. Nice touches: The main dining room features an enclosed greenhouse addition for lovely garden-side dining.

Watson's Merion Inn

n 1885, Patrick Collins opened up a "fine marine boarding villa, convenient to the Iron Pier and the big hotels". It was a first class establishment. By 1900, it evolved from Collins' Cottage to Collins' Cafe, a rakish Irish bar featuring whiskies, seafood, Milwaukee beers and "neatly appointed rooms for ladies". Andrew Zillinger purchased the business and changed its name to "The Merion." Mr. Zillinger, who was the chief steward of the Merion Cricket Club, was rumored to have received financial backing from some of the club members to assure themselves a "high class retreat" in fashionable Cape May. At The Merion, additional rooms on the second floor were converted for dining; an outdoor beer garden was added with, of course, a separate entrance for ladies.

Throughout the following years, The Merion continued its success under a number of owners. In 1970, Warren Watson purchased the inn and to this day, the 96 year tradition of simple, good food continues. In the beginning, Watson divided his restaurant duties with school teaching. Today, he personally devotes all his time to the demanding chores of running a successful restaurant. His staff is a loyal crew of locals who return year after year to effectively and courteously host, bartend, cook, serve and clean up. Chef Willie Robinson is in the kitchen where small considerations, such as fresh-slicing the cole slaw and using real whipped cream to top the pies, have made this establishment a notable eatery.

Because of Watson's fine reputation, one can expect a wait. Nevertheless, the interim time can be spent pleasantly enough sipping cocktails under a canopied outdoor cafe. On the inside, one can lean elbows on an exquisite solid cherry bar, signed and dated in 1904, featuring fluted oak columns and beveled mirrors.

A subtly lit, mellow atmosphere is carried throughout the several intimate rooms and the larger enclosed porch, all of which retain the feeling of dining in a private home. The walls are filled with the owner's private collection of fine period paintings in elaborate gilded frames. There are romantic oil portraits and landscapes, watercolors, "Gibson Girl" drawings and formal animal paintings. The original exterior window frames have been fitted with shelves and filled with old South Jersey glass, handcarved decoys, antique china pieces and plants.

Once seated at a carefully arranged table, complete with candles and fresh flowers, and the choice of a meal is made, the parade of taste treats begins. Appetizers are traditional with a few surprises. On a lucky day, the soup du jour might be a rich Snapper or a superb Manhattan Clam Chowder. Order a cup instead of a bowl to assure room for the complimentary relish tray which includes a *heavenly* cream-coleslaw. The homemade dinner bread is a thick crusted marble-rye, sometimes nestled in with tiny fruit-filled muffins.

Pristinely-pure seafood entrees are broiled, sauteed, deep-fried or baked to perfection and served in generous portions. Fish specialties are varied according to the freshest available at the time. Along with the standards of flounder, shrimp, scallops and backfin crab, the selection has included swordfish, weakfish, bluefish, drum fish and whatever else may be running locally! The pride of the kitchen is a stuffed lobster with its magnificent meat taken out in chunks, blended with lump crabmeat, delicately seasoned, then replaced in its shell and broiled. There's a choice medley of six veal dishes, each individually prepared with the delicate tastes of white or red wines combined with lemon or mushrooms; the cutlets dipped in egg and lightly breaded are a melt-in-your-mouth dish. For a meal that reminds you of Mom and home, try the juicy sauteed sliced leg of veal. Vegetables are *strictly* fresh and are cooked at staggered times and in small amounts to assure crispness. Lively combinations such as honeyglazed carrots with cashews, baked string beans parmesan or garden vegetables marinated in a unique vinegarette sauce are truly superb and are deservedly served separately. The "Merion Potatoe Cup" is blended with sour cream and chives, topped with cheese and baked in a casserole cup.

Service at Watson's is prompt and attentive, yet not pressing. A meal can be eaten leisurely—and wisely so, because the desserts should not be missed. Sinfully rich banana cream pies are baked daily and served with real whipped cream. A classic shortcake is hard to resist with a choice of fresh strawberries, blueberries or peaches that reflect the pickings of nearby farms—with more of that whipped cream topping. There's also New York Cheesecake, native fruit glazed pies and parfaits made to order.

Many, many meals have been served within the walls of this neat and trim building at 106 Decatur Street. Through years of prohibition, depression, some quiet times to follow, the motel boom and finally Cape May's revitalization in its historic preservation movement, the Merion Inn has endured. To this day, it successfully continues a tradition of serving customers fresh seafood, meats, vegetables and fruits of local origin, with the highest standards of preparation and service.

WATSON'S MERION INN, 106 Decatur Street, Cape May, N.J. 08204; (609) 884-8363. Warren Watson, owner. A traditional-style restaurant housed in a vintage Victorian building, serving the public since 1885. Open May through September. Open weekends in April and October. Dinners and cocktails served 4:30 to 10 pm. No reservations taken. Early Diners Special available to those seated before 6 pm.

Restaurant Maureen
∽
Upstairs at Gloria's

acing the ocean on the west corner of Decatur Street the exterior of this three story building has virtually remained unchanged in its 103 years of existence. Rumored to be a drinking and gambling saloon during Prohibition, it posed as a bathhouse with overnight lodging. The structure was located directly opposite Cape May's famous Iron Pier, which stretched out into the Atlantic to meet the steamboats coming in from the Delaware Bay.

In a pronounced contrast to Gloria's rock & roll saloon and deli-restaurant downstairs, Gloria's Upstairs has recently made some great changes by graciously sharing her quarters with a new girl in town: Restaurant Maureen of Philadelphian fame has moved in. Chef-owner Stephen Horn, his wife (for whom the restaurant is named), and a complete staff of 13, has relocated for the summer to their new historical address in Cape May.

Considering the success of Maureen in Philadelphia since 1977 and the excellent reviews given by *Gourmet, Cuisine, Bon Appetite* and other international food and wine magazines, this establishment should prove to be a welcome addition to Cape May's eclectic dining scene.

Stephen Horn has been cooking professionally for nine years and has studied at Cordon Blue in Paris. The creative cooking at Maureen is based on Chef Horn's training in haute cuisine and his contemporary style of food preparation.

Guests for dinner are seated in the elegant dining oasis on the 2nd floor, complete with an open balcony offering a panoramic view of the Atlantic Ocean. Inside, the atmosphere is pure elegance with crystal chandeliers, flickering candles, and tables topped with crisp white linens. A rose and green color scheme is repeated throughout, from the Persian floral rug, wallpaper and drapes, to the painted ceiling medallions.

Newcomers to Maureen will be in for an exciting culinary experience beginning with the list of hot and cold appetizers. Start off with Pasta Gorgonzola; delicate spinach noodles in a cream sauce lightly flavored with Gorgonzola cheese and sweet green peas, or try the Scallop Seviche; chilled sea scallops, sliced and served in a lemon-spicy marinade. Another excellent appetizer with a charming touch is Oyster Maureen; oysters poached in a lemony-butter sauce, crowned with pearls of caviar and served with an icy flute of champagne.

All entrees on the menu are served as full dinners, which includes a tasty salad of romaine lettuce and fresh mushrooms in a mustard-vinaigrette dressing and a choice of two vegetables.

Flown-in seafood plays a major role on the list of fare. An enticing main course is Dover Dieppoise, real Dover Sole served in a light wine and cream sauce, seasoned with mussels and shrimp. More favorites of the Chef include Roast Island Duck, with a surprising flavor counterpoint of fresh strawberries, and Medallions of Veal served on a bed of lobster, shrimp and crab, complimented with a sauce of St. Milo. Shrimp a la Marseille is tenderly sauteed with green peppercorns and leek, in a sauce of cream, Tarragon and garlic. A good part in the success of the dishes here, is the result of Horn's accomplished *buerre blanc* type sauces, which make these entrees exceptional.

To end the meal, there is a fine selection of desserts made daily on the premises by a specialized pastry chef. Selections include a delicious Chocolate Praline Torte and Creme Courvoissier—a cool brandy-flavored custard. Apricot tart, topped with mint sherbet is another unusually good combination. There are also such delec-tables as Creme Caramels, White Chocolate Mousse and a memor-able Strawberry Genoise—a French vanilla marzipan cake.

A frequently changed selection of wines from France and California are available.

Seasoned and new guests of Restaurant Maureen ∞ Upstairs at Gloria's are in for a full measure of treats. This is an eatery to be admired both visually and for its totally enjoyable cuisine.

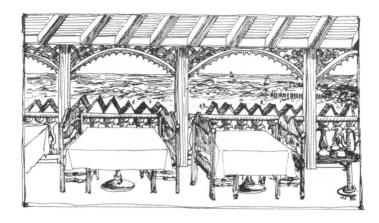

RESTAURANT MAUREEN ∞ UPSTAIRS AT GLORIA'S. Decatur Street at the Beach, Cape May, N.J. 08204; (609) 884-3774. Jay Barnes, owner. An historic 103 year old Victorian structure housing Gloria's—a Deli-Bar with live music daily and nightly, and an elegant upper level dining room and balcony, featuring the original nouvelle cuisine of Restaurant Maureen. Stephen and Maureen Horn, Chef and host. Cocktails served in a second floor Victorian bar adjoining the dining room. Full dinners and additional Chef specialties are served at Maureen, 7 days a week, from 5 pm. There is a minimum entree price per person of $13.95. Open May 10 to September 20.

The Chalfonte

he Chalfonte, alive and well at 107 years old, stands as a living testimony to Cape May's tradition of fine hotels and southern hospitality. Set back from the ocean, as well as several blocks away from the heart of the historical district, the Chalfonte remains the only major hotel to survive the fire of 1878 which burned down 30 or more acres of Cape May's finest landmarks.

The very roots of this hotel, so well-known for its southern hospitality, were historically associated with the deep South in a somewhat ironic way: the Chalfonte was built by Henry Sawyer, a Union soldier who was released from a Confederate prison in exchange for the son of the famous General Robert E. Lee. (This Confederate-Union prisoner exchange was arranged by President Lincoln.)

The Chalfonte still caters to many generations of southerners, who return to their "second home" year after year. The family atmosphere has remained and endured all the pressures of 20th century "progress" through the perseverence of the loyal Satterfield family who have been the owners since 1910. Several years ago, Mary Satterfield, 87, entrusted the management to Judy Bartella and Anne Le Duc, who amazingly keep things running well throughout the 103 room hotel from early summer to early fall. During the winter, both women teach school.

There is an unmistakable feeling of nostalgia here. Guests can quickly float into the past as they wander down the long hallways, passing by dozens of louvre-doors leading to each simply furnished guestroom. The canopied veranda is wide and of the wrap-around variety, filled with wooden and wicker rocking chairs and patrons of all ages. There are lacey balconies facing the ocean, and tall columns topped with gingerbread, arching their way up to the third floor.

Meals are included in the price of a room, but the public can join hotel guests in the dining room for a southern-cooked breakfast and dinner that is homemade and prepared from scratch by Helen Dickerson. A Chalfonte tradition in her own right, Helen, 72, and her family have been cooking here for four generations. Mother Dickerson started it all, and Helen herself began as a babysitter for the owners when she was eight. Later, she worked as a waitress, head waitress and finally head cook. Today, Helen's daughter, Dot Burton, is her chief assistant and even Dot's husband and children are involved in preparing the two meals a day for as many as 180 guests, when there's a full house.

In the huge restored Victorian dining room, topped with large ceiling fans, the atmosphere is old-fashioned and formal by shore standards. Jackets are required for the men at dinnertime, and children under 7 dine in a separate room under the watchful eye of a staff member. The menu is a Satterfield original and hasn't changed much over the years. Recipes are tried and true—some at least 50 years old. A Virginia Country Breakfast each morning includes fresh fruit juice, eggs, bacon, a chunk of crunchy deep-fried fish, a big bowl of spoonbread (which tastes like a combination of cornbread pudding and egg-custard), piping hot homemade bisquits, coffee and milk. On Sunday, a specialty of Kidney Stew is also served.

Southern dinners vary with the day of the week: Monday, it's Herbed Roast Leg of Lamb; Roast Beef on Tuesday; Fried Chicken on Wednesday; Baked Virginia Ham or Roast Turkey on Thursday; Deviled Crab and Bluefish on Friday; Saturday is usually Roast Beef night and Sunday afternoon, dinner is Helen's famous Southern Broiled or Fried Chicken. Dinner starts with a soup of the day, such as creamy mushroom flavored with nutmeg or a clear tangy onion-filled broth. All the trimmings are served family style, and a waitress will start passing platters filled with ears of white corn, buttery giant lima beans, hot popover rolls and baked Jersey tomatoes stuffed with chopped onions and buttered breadcrumbs. The vegetables are Jersey fresh. Some other wonderful taste treats which have accompanied dinners are carrots in a light syrup; an eggplant casserole layered with breadcrumbs, onions and tomatoes, topped with cheese; and a delicately sliced and steamed cabbage dish.

The food is plentiful and most guests have trouble squeezing in the dessert. So Helen has prepared something that can slide down easily after a full meal—a small dollop of ice cream served with chocolate syrup and whipped cream. Sometimes Dot's baking shows up alongside—perhaps chocolate devil's food or a crispy apple cobbler. Children dining here in August probably will be visited by Mr. Conklin, an elderly gentleman and one of the Chalfonte's regular clientele, who loves to surprise the little ones with a lollipop treat—"if they eat up all their dinner".

For those who want to try southern cooking a la Helen Dickerson at home, a newly-published cookbook with lots of delicious original recipes is available in the hotel lobby.

The Chalfonte is a grand old lady who survives the changes of the 19th and 20th centuries by preserving age-old traditions and catering to those loyal clientele who keep returning each year. Dining here is a remarkable change from the "rush-you-in and rush-you-out" variety so prevalent today.

On the way out, don't forget to rest for a bit on the veranda to savour the meal—and maybe some of your own early memories, when time didn't move quite so fast.

THE CHALFONTE, 301 Howard Street, Cape May, N.J. 08204; (609) 884-8409. Judy Bartella and Anne Le Duc, Innkeepers. A Victorian Hotel with significant architectural style, listed on the National Register of Historic Places. Open June 10 to September 12 (open weekends late in season). One hundred and three guestrooms with shared and private baths. Accommodation rates include breakfast and dinner. Dining room and King Edward Room Bar open to the public daily. (For accommodation rates, meal/bar time and prices, see Rates and Schedule, Index of Inns).

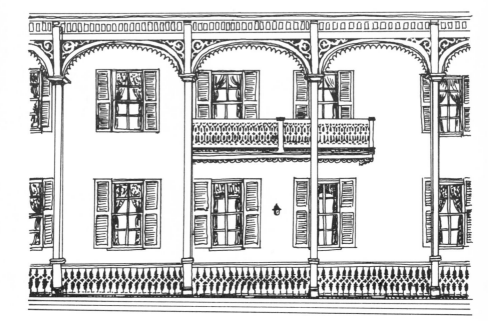

 # The Mad Batter

here's something extremely pleasant about eating in the fresh open air, amidst ocean breezes and sunshine. Here is a rare and wonderful eatery with enough room to offer customers the luxury of a leisurely meal without pressing them to go. Such are the enticements of The Mad Batter restaurant located at The Carroll Villa Hotel, an 1875 Victorian structure dripping with three stories of gingerbread and still renting rooms to vacationing tourists.

Seven years ago, new owners Harry Kulkowitz and Vickie Seitchik had somewhat of a white elephant on their hands. Enthusiastic to make a go at an existing but waning business, they were saddled to a rundown rooming house, with a large, gloomy dining room and a bare porch which was too sunny for comfortable eating alfresco. Something had to be done, but before any exterior changes were made, the owners had to secure approval of the township's hard-nosed historical commission. Luckily, a bit of research uncovered an original photo of the Carroll Villa facade sporting those absolutely necessary awnings to shield vacationing Victorians from the sun. With proof in hand, Vickie and Harry promptly installed a grand striped awning of their own, and to brighten up the spacious dining room, several ceiling skylights were put in—success at last!

While functioning in a wonderful Victorian building, The Mad Batter exerts its own style, combining three distinct dining areas. A generous expanse of front porch is just a step up from the sidewalk. Here customers breakfast and brunch, European style, under that jaunty yellow canopy. Animated at all times, the whole intimate cafe setting—with its splash of color overhead, white cloth-covered tables and glimpses of the sparkling blue Atlantic—is straight out of a French Impressionist painting. On the inside is the original hotel dining room—its Victorian past still evident in the high beamed ceilings, windows lined with lacy curtains, oak tables, antique caned chairs and a wide exposure of shiny hardwood floor. Old world charm mingles with modern paintings, photographs and prints; reminders of Harry's days as an art dealer. The skylights are another unexpected bow to the 20th century and the room exudes a style befitting its nouvelle cuisine.

Most recently, a backyard area was transformed into yet another open-air dining spot. The atmosphere is garden-terrace complete with flower beds, a small pond, and a commissioned marble statue by artist Sally McInerney. An overhead canopy dips down just enough to cleverly block out the view of neighboring backyards.

Originally, Harry and Vickie intended for their restaurant to specialize in crepes—thus the name, The Mad Batter. Somehow, the long list of crepes and pancake dishes developed into an elaborate menu devised by Harry and his first head cook, Dennis Finley. The kitchen here is serious, with a staff of young talented chefs, actively supported by the management. Currently there's Jean Lloyd, Joanne McIntyre and Chris Bannon responsible for breakfast and brunch; George Pechin, Mindy Silver and Joseph Lotozo are the dinner chefs.

In addition to the diversified menu, which accounts for a good part of The Mad Batter's success, a huge blackboard in each dining area lists the specials of the day.

As soon as the weather allows, many customers opt for breakfast or brunch on that wonderful front porch. Morning openers offer enough selections to suit anyone's mood or appetite. There are freshly-squeezed orange, apple, celery and carrot juices, homemade lemon buttermilk bread and croissants. This is probably the only place in town to offer fat pumpernickel bagels, spinach latkes and breakfast health foods, such as porridge with raisins and nuts or honey granola topped with fresh strawberries, blueberries *and* bananas. Special egg dishes are baked or poached, served with English muffins and topped with a choice of vegetable, meats and sauces. If one hasn't "gone bananas" in deciding what to choose from the incredible menu, try the griddle cakes of the same name, which is loaded with fresh bananas, creme anglaise and banana liqueur!

For late-risers or a more substantial luncheon-hour meal, there are some well prepared dishes with inventive combinations, such as the Chicken Salad in Melon; cold, marinated Spicy Game Hen and a number of special Smoked Meat and Fish Platters (these freshly-smoked on the premises).

Salads are substantial enough to be ordered as a luncheon dish. A good clean taste is the fresh spinach, nestled with sweet orange sections, croutons and topped with a creamy vinaigrette dressing. For the more adventurous, try the Indonesian Salad which has a marvelous contrast of soft and crunchy morsels—brown rice, raisins, scallions and celery, studded with water chestnuts, sesame seeds and cashews,—all tossed with a tangy oriental dressing.

As evening falls, the slates are wiped clean and a new dinner menu appears—one that changes every two weeks, to insure constant variety. The Mad Batter thrives on variety and change—Vickie reveals plans for a complete baking facility on the premises and the expansion of their entire breakfast, lunch and dinner menus to now include a selection of gourmet Chinese and Oriental dishes. Pasta, from fettucini to wontons, will be homemade. And to get first-hand experience at the subtleties of Asian cooking and seasoning, Harry and Vickie and their cooks made a special trip to the Far East this past winter!

A typical evening's fare can start off with a Mad Batter favorite— Zuppa de Clams, an appetizer of clams delicately cooked in an Italian herb sauce. Soups here are a house specialty—the mushroom has an intense flavor and an almost pureed texture; the clam chowder is rich and chunky with bacon, onions and heavy cream.

The salads are consistently good and perk up the taste buds with unexpected combinations and delightful dressings—the Thai Salad is a hearty chef's salad transformed into an exotic treat by mating its ingredients with a wonderful peanut-creme dressing with just enough nut flavor, a hint of chili powder for spice and a sprinkling of unfamiliar, but delicious, lacey-woven chips on top.

Entrees of chicken, seafood, beef and pork dishes appear on the menu; each baked, broiled or sauteed with enticing vegetables and complimentary sauces. An excellent dish is the Stuffed Loin of Pork—tender slices of pork with hints of garlic, broiled in whiskey and served with wafer-thin slices of fresh, firm zucchini and diced potatoes that nicely round off the pungent flavor of the meat.

A variety of imaginative desserts are prepared with love, and absolutely no attention to calories. The chocolate numbers are decadent—a very rich Black Velvet mousse encased in vanilla sponge cake goes down with no regrets. The Royal Vienna Walnut Torte triples layers of chocolate and nuts and tops it all with a brandied brown sugar buttermilk icing. How can one resist desserts with names like Loreen's Original Sin and Queen of Sheba cake? On a lighter note, there are fresh fruit tarts, dessert crepes and homemade icecreams. The exotic fresh fruit sherbets, whipped with liqueurs, are a perfect blend of an after dinner cordial and dessert. Bottomless cups of Mocha Java/Columbian coffee or herbal teas are available, as well as popular Perrier, sparkling cider and homemade lemonade.

The Mad Batter is a commendable establishment with a four-star reputation and consistently excellent reviews. Entrees are planned daily to insure variety and freshness. Service is admittedly slow— the kitchen cooks everything to order. Along with the wonderful innovative food, the restaurant has all the necessary desirable qualities: it is casual, intimate, bistro-like and friendly, with a natural camaraderie between patrons. It is a place to be taken personally.

THE MAD BATTER RESTAURANT, The Carrol Villa Hotel, 19 Jackson Street, Cape May, N.J. 08204; (609) 884-5970. Harry Kulkowitz and Vickie Sietchik, owners and hosts. A 19th century restored hotel and restaurant serving gourmet breakfast, brunch and dinner. Open early April thru mid-October. Breakfast and brunch served from 8 a.m. to 2:30 p.m. Dinner served from 5:30 to 10 p.m. No alcoholic beverages served; guests may bring their own at a service charge of 50¢ per person for glasses and ice. Moderately priced guestroom accommodations with shared or private bath, one-half block from ocean.

Author's Note

To those seasoned visitors of Cape May, it is obvious that one of the city's tiniest and most popular restaurants is missing from this guidebook.

In explanation, the proprietors of this establishment have voiced a fear of becoming inundated due to the extra publicity, and in all fairness to their loyal customers, they have opted to remain anonymous.

As authors, we feel our deserving readers are entitled to know that this omission is not an oversight on our part.

The food served here is near perfection. A brief description is in order: pasta is made daily on the premises; fish comes fresh from Cape May docks; herbs used here are grown in the owners' garden. Everything about this restaurant is honest and its food is fresh, healthful and creatively prepared from appetizers such as avocado with walnuts and herbs to entrees such as homemade fettucine with pesto/basil sauce.

Local fruits and chocolate often end the meal—wild Blackberry Mousse, Chocolate Mousse with Grand Marnier, fresh raspberries with cassis and cream, or Walnut Blackbottom Pie are some typical dessert fare.

Honor compels us not to reveal the name and address of this extremely successful restaurant, but if you should stay at one of the guesthouses we've described here, chances are our innkeeping friends will direct you right to the doorstep.

 # Alternate Accommodations

Due to the increasing popularity of the guesthouse/bed & breakfast type of accommodation in Cape May, we have included the following pleasant alternatives as a service to our readers. *Based on personal recommendations*, the following establishments offer the traveler a variety of accommodations ranging from modest to elegant. Several family-style apartment rentals, available for extended stays, have also been included. For additional details and rates, call or write to the inn of your choice.

NEW!

Abigail Adams
12 Jackson Street
884-1371
Guestrooms—Bed & Breakfast
Donna and Ed Misner

The Manor House
612 Hughes Street
884-4710
Guestrooms—Bed & Breakfast
Spurgeon and Joyce Smith

The Albert G. Stevens House
127 Myrtle Avenue
884-4717
Guestrooms—Bed & Breakfast
Dean Krumrine and Dick Flynn

Alexander's
653 Washington Street
884-2555
Guestrooms—Bed & Breakfast
Larry and Diane Muentz

The Bedford Inn
805 Stockton Avenue
884-4158
Guestrooms and Apartments
Cindy and Alan Schmucker

The Carroll Villa
19 Jackson Street
884-9619
Guestrooms
Harry Kulkowitz and Vickie Seitchik

The Columbia House
26 Ocean Street
884-2789
Apartments (guestrooms in off season)
Roger Crawford and Maggie Fenton

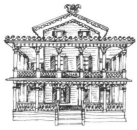

The Delsea
621 Columbia Avenue
884-8540
Guestrooms
Suzanne Littell and Rosemary Stumpo

The Mooring
801 Stockton Street
884-5425
Guestrooms and Apartments
Richard and Carolyn Detrick

The Summer Cottage
613 Columbia Avenue
884-4948
Guestrooms—Bed & Breakfast
Nancy and Bill Rishforth

The Twin Gables
731 Columbia Avenue
884-7332
Guestrooms
Tony Bevivino

he 19th century charm of Cape May is perhaps most intense when the summer crowds have gone and the town returns to its quiet Victorian village atmosphere.

It is obvious why the entire town has been designated a National Historic Landmark. The visual qualities of its architectural heritage takes moments to discover, yet days to explore. Weekend walking tours of the historic district continue, weather permitting, through most of the winter.

Late October marks a high-point for Victorian-lovers. Cape May's Victorian Weekend, offers four days of museum and house tours, as well as a variety of activities designed to give the visitor a taste of by-gone era.

This year there has been a concerted effort by a number of year 'round innkeepers and mall merchants to promote the small-town, Christmas season charm of Cape May with special holiday events. "Cottages at Christmastime" features a tour of four Victorian Inns (The Queen Victoria, Captain Mey's Inn, The Victorian Rose and The Brass Bed), all decorated for the Yule Season. Guests of the Queen Victoria can go "Wassailing and Warbling" during one weekend stay or listen to Dickens' readings and literary discussions at another.

The Washington Street Mall offers a candlelight walk for shoppers, with strolling carollers and a wine and cheese treat in the gift shops. There are also special seasonal theatrical and choir performances.

A fitting end to the season is the annual Christmas Candlelight House Tour, sponsored by the Mid-Atlantic Center for the Arts. This extremely popular event gives the visitor an opportunity to tour the historic interior of the Emlen Physick Estate as well as a number of private homes, Victorian guesthouses and churches all festively decorated for the holidays.

Rates and Schedule
Index of Inns

Daily rates are quoted for two persons per individual guestroom/suite. There may be an additional charge for extra person(s) in room. Single travelers should inquire for special rates. Families traveling with children please check with individual inn for child-accommodation policies.

In general, guesthouses do *not* accept credit-cards, but will accept personal checks in payment. A deposit is generally required to hold a reservation.

Note the following abbreviations:

Δ	=	inns open all year
B&B	=	bed and breakfast. Rates include full or continental breakfast
L.O.S.R.	=	lower off season rates.

The Abbey, B&B, open Apr. 6-Oct. 30, Sun. to Sun. - 10% discount, $50. to $80. L.O.S.R.

Alexander's, B&B and Restaurant, open Apr.-Dec., $68. with private bath, $50. to $57. with shared bath and sink in each room.

The Barnard-Good House, B&B, open Apr. 1-Nov., Sun. to Sun. 10% discount, $52. to $73.

Δ **The Brass Bed,** B&B, $45. to $57. with shared bath, $65. with private bath. Weekly discount. L.O.S.R.

Δ **Captain Mey's Inn,** B&B, $50. to $75. L.O.S.R.

The Carroll Villa Hotel (Mad Batter Restaurant), open Apr.-Nov., $44. to $48 with private bath, $30. to $36. with shared bath. L.O.S.R.

The Chalfonte Hotel, open June-Sept. (Open weekends late in season) Singles daily $39. to $53. Weekly $224. to $305. Double (without bath) daily $69. to $88. Weekly $397. to $506. Double (with bath) daily $96. to $98. Weekly $552. to $564. Lower rates in June, early July and Fall weekends. Dining room open to the public. Breakfast served daily 8:30-10 a.m., $5.95. Dinner, Mon. through Sat., 6:30-8:30 p.m., $12.95. *Men required to wear jackets to dinner only.* King Edward Bar open 5 p.m.-1 a.m. daily.

Δ **The Dormer House International,** rates adjusted according to month and specific apartment. $175. to $485. weekly and $28. to $79. daily.

The Duke of Windsor Inn, B&B, Open Apr. 1-Oct. 30, seven nights-one night free. $40. to $60. L.O.S.R.

Δ **The Gingerbread House,** B&B, $52. to $75., L.O.S.R.

Δ **The Hanson House,** B&B, $45. to $75. Lower weekly rates. L.O.S.R.

Δ **The Holly House,** $35. to $45. Lower weekly rates.

The Humphrey Hughes House, B&B, open mid-Apr. to Mid-Oct., $45. to $90.

The Mainstay Inn and The Cottage, B&B, open Apr. 1-Nov., $44. to $78.

Poor Richard's Inn, open Apr. 1-Oct. 30, $34. to $57. Apartments $315. to $465 per week. L.O.S.R.

Δ **The Queen Victoria,** B&B, $48. to $58. with shared bath, $84. with private bath and small refrigerators. L.O.S.R.

Δ **The Seventh Sister,** Jan. to Mar.-$35., Apr.-$38., May-$42., Jun.-$45, July & Aug.-$49., Sept.-$45., Oct.-$42., Nov. & Dec.-$38. 5% discount for week's stay. L.O.S.R.

Δ **The Victorian Rose,** B&B, $40. to $80. Apartments $300. to $350. per week. Innlet Cottage $375. to $475. per week. L.O.S.R.

Δ **The Windward House,** B&B, $45. to $65. Efficiency apartment available year round. $40. per day off season - $300. to $350. per week June to Sept. L.O.S.R.

New Jersey born, bred and educated, authors Marsha Cudworth and Howard Michaels discovered a mutual love for Cape May. As artists, they were drawn to the 19th century charm of the town, at first painting and photographing the numerous examples of Victorian architecture. Subsequently, they decided to collaborate on the production of a guidebook featuring fine examples of restored guesthouses and restaurants.

Currently, the authors live in a small South Jersey community. Marsha Cudworth teaches elementary art in a public school and has designed craft projects featured in *Family Circle*, *American Girl* and *McCall's* magazines. Her *Incredible Inedible* © bread-dough ornaments are sold in specialty gift shops.

Howard Michaels taught secondary art for two years in New South Wales, Australia. After returning to the United States from an extended tour of the South Pacific, he re-entered the art field as a free-lance photographer and artist.

NEW!

SELF-GUIDED ARCHITECTURAL TOURS OF CAPE MAY, N.J. This one-of-a-kind handbook is a must for all visitors to Cape May, providing a beautifully illustrated guide to Cape May's Victorian treasures. Walking, auto and bike tours feature 127 architectural points of interest — restored B & B inns, hotels, commercial structures and private residences. Includes a glossary of architectural terms and styles, detailed street maps and a concise history of Cape May and Cape May Point.

Copies of *Self-Guided Architectural Tours* ($6.95) and *Victorian Holidays* ($7.95) can be ordered direct through the distributor. Please add $1.00 for postage and handling for each book ordered (N.J. residents add 6% sales tax). Make check payable to Bric-A-Brac Bookworks, Box 887, Forked River, New Jersey 08731.

Acknowledgements

For sharing their individual expertise, we wish to express our gratitude to the following very special people: John Cudworth Jr., loan of recording equipment; Helen DeMauro, proofreading and typing manuscripts; Kathleen Naughton, editing; Harvey Phillips of Phillips Photo Illustrators, Colt's Neck, N.J., photographic consultant; Debi Scalera of Gemini Graphics, Montclair, N.J., graphic consultant; The Chris Sooy Swing Band, providing music to unwind by after days of research in Cape May, and lastly Alan Wojtowicz, graphic production advisor.

We are especially proud of the aesthetic presence of this edition and give thanks and recognition to the following: Nick Solovioff, for granting permission to use his lovely painting of the Chalfonte Hotel; Elaine Silverman, for the use of her charming Mad Batter/Carroll Villa drawing; The Mid-Atlantic Center for the Arts (MAC), for the use of historical illustrations from the Physick Estate Library and Marj Forrester of *The Victorian Look*, Cape May, N.J., for assistance in securing Victorian reproduction wallpaper used in our cover design.

For the historical introduction to this edition, we are indebted to the numerous well-written magazine and newspaper articles as well as promotional brochures printed about Cape May; our enlightening interviews with each proprietor, and MAC's informative and entertaining walking tours, taken with innkeepers Bruce Minnix (The Holly House) and Jay Schatz (The Abbey). Major book references used for historical material are credited to *Ho! For Cape Island* by Robert Crozier Alexander and *This is Cape May—A Visitor's Guide* by Jean T. Timmons and Donald P. Timmons.

A special thanks is given to all the proprietors of the establishments included in this book, for sharing their personal stories with us and for their enthusiastic support throughout our project.

The Authors